DERIVATIVES
DECODED

Edna Carew

DERIVATIVES
DECODED

ALLEN & UNWIN

First published in 1995
Allen & Unwin Pty Ltd
9 Atchison Street, St Leonards, NSW 2065 Australia

National Library of Australia
Cataloguing-in-Publication entry:

Carew, Edna, 1949– .
  Derivatives decoded.

  Includes index.
  ISBN 1 86373 905 X.

  1. Derivative securities. I. Title.

332.632

Set in 10.5/13.5 pt Palatino by DOCUPRO, Sydney
Printed by Australian Print Group, Maryborough, Victoria

10 9 8 7 6 5 4 3 2 1

CONTENTS

· · · · · · · · · · · · · ·

TABLES

FIGURES

ACKNOWLEDGEMENTS

· ·

Writing a book about a subject as important as derivatives—so important that it will remain central to the operations of the world's financial markets—would be impossible without the help of many people who have been generous with their time, energy, enthusiasm and specialist knowledge.

Merely saying 'thank you' seems an inadequate acknowledgement of their contributions; I can only hope that they understand how much I value them.

I particularly thank those who commented on chapters and helped with technical details: Stephen Chambers, Jeff Duncan-Nagy, Marianne Gizycki, Graham Gordon, John Hutchinson, Geoff Kelly, Bob Mackintosh, Warwick Morris, Paul Robertson, Malcolm Rodgers, David Rowe, Peter Stebbing, Ian Town, James Watts, Jeremy Weir, Simon Wright.

And those who helped with specific sections of text: Pat Apperson, John Bird, Tricia Bowden, Geoff Bowmer, Rahoul Chowdry, John Duggan, Lucio Febo, Lincoln Gould, Ian Hastings, Peter Ho, Tony Hunter, Ian Moore, Michael Ormaechea, Philip Pyle, Bob Rankin, John Rutherford, John Shanahan, Brett Stevenson, Kevin Stevenson, Andrew Stewart, Ken Sue, Frank Traczewski, Steven Wood.

I am also grateful to the many others interviewed who generously gave time and information. These include Les Hosking and David White, and the staff of the Sydney Futures Exchange and ASX Derivatives.

Thanks of course to Patrick Gallagher for the suggestion of a book on derivatives.

John Hoffmann's editing skills were helpful and supportive as always, as was John Iremonger's enthusiasm for the project. Those two claim a clearer knowledge of derivatives, having been in close contact with the production of this book. I hope that many more will find in it the same illumination.

Edna Carew
Sydney
March 1995

LEARNING THE LANGUAGE
· ·

ABBREVIATIONS

AFMA	Australian Financial Markets Association
APPI	Asian Petroleum Price Index
ASX	Australian Stock Exchange
ASXD	ASX Derivatives
CBOE	Chicago Board Options Exchange
CBOT	Chicago Board of Trade
CME	Chicago Mercantile Exchange
Comex	Commodity Exchange Inc of New York
CSCE	Coffee, Sugar & Cocoa Exchange (New York)
IMM	International Monetary Market (division of the CME)
IPE	International Petroleum Exchange of London
ISDA	International Swaps and Derivatives Association
KLCE	Kuala Lumpur Commodity Exchange
LBMA	London Bullion Market Association
LIFFE-	London International Financial Futures Exchange and
LTOM	London Traded Options Market
LME	London Metals Exchange
MATIF	*Marché à Terme International de France*
MONEP	*Marché des Options Négociables de la Bourse de Paris*
NZFOE	New Zealand Futures and Options Exchange
NYCE	New York Cotton Exchange
NYFE	New York Futures Exchange
NYMEX	New York Mercantile Exchange
PHLX	Philadelphia Stock Exchange

SFE   Sydney Futures Exchange
SFECH   Sydney Futures Exchange Clearing House
SIMEX   Singapore International Monetary Exchange
TGE   Tokyo Grain Exchange
TIFFE   Tokyo International Financial Futures Exchange
TOCOM   Tokyo Commodity Exchange
TSE   Tokyo Stock Exchange

ABAFRA terms   terms and conditions applying to forward-rate agreements (FRAs), recommended by the $A forward-rate agreements working party of banks and merchant banks operating under the auspices of the Australian Bankers' Association (ABA). ABAFRA terms have been replaced by Aussie ISDA. See **Aussie ISDA**.

accreting principal swap   a swap whose notional principal increases (whereas with conventional swaps the notional principle is static). Also accumulation swap.

adjustable long-term puttable securities   see **dual currency bond**. *Abbrev.* **ALPS**.

AFMA   *abbrev.* **Australian Financial Markets Association**.

algorithm   borrowed from the jargon of computer science, at its simplest an algorithm is a series of formulae—a model—used to solve a problem. The Black–Scholes option pricing model is an example of an algorithm used in financial markets.

all-or-nothing option   an option whose payoff is predetermined if the underlying asset or index is at or beyond the strike price when the option expires. The value of the payoff is unaffected by the difference between the underlying and the strike price. Also *binary option, digital option*. See **payoff**.

All-Ordinaries Share Price Riskless Index Notes   notes securitising the price movement in Australian domestic share prices, as represented by the All-Ordinaries index, over the term of the notes. Designed by Bankers Trust Australia Ltd. Also *protected equity notes. Abbrev.* **ASPRIN**.

alligator spread   a position whose spread is so large it 'eats' the client (chews up the client's cash).

ALPS   *abbrev.* **adjustable long-term puttable securities**.

alternative option   an option on the return of the best call or worst put from two or more securities or indexes during a specified period. Also *better-of-two-assets option*.

American option   a put or call option that is tradeable and can be exercised at any time up to the date it is due to expire. The options most commonly traded on the Sydney Futures Exchange and on the Australian Stock Exchange's options market are examples of an American option. See **European option**.

amortising cap   an interest-rate cap covering decreasing notional principal amounts which usually reflect repayment of the principal of an underlying instrument.

amortising collar   an interest-rate collar covering decreasing notional principal amounts.

amortising option   an interest-rate option covering decreasing notional principal amounts.

amortising swap   an interest-rate swap with a decreasing principal amount. Preferably the amortisation schedule of the swap takes place at the same rate as the amortisation of the underlying instrument, otherwise a fixed-rate receiver risks pre-payment or extension.

annuity swap   a swap involving an initial payment or receipt then an exchange of equal coupons during the life of the swap.

APT   *abbrev.* **automated pit trading**.

arbitrage   to take advantage of different rates, prices or conditions between different markets or maturities. Arbitragers make the most of inconsistencies between prices in different markets, for example if a stock sells for a lower price in one market than in another, an arbitrager would buy it at the lower price and sell it at the higher. Pure (riskless) arbitrage involves no risk, eg, trading foreign exchange forward while borrowing in one currency, trading it spot and investing in a foreign currency. See **risk arbitrage**.

arrears swap   see **in-arrears swap**.

Asian option   see **average price or rate option**.

ASPRIN   *abbrev.* **All-Ordinaries Share Price Riskless Index Notes**.

asset-backed security   a financial instrument securitised by an asset or assets such as property, a mortgage or credit-card receivables.

asset-based swap   a swap where the fixed payment stream of the swap is generated by an asset, eg, a bond, held by a party to the swap. A fixed-for-floating interest-rate swap.

at-market order   see **market order**.

at the money   a term used in option trading to describe an exercise (or strike) price that is at or about current market levels. See **in the money, out of the money**.

Atlantic option   see **Bermuda option**.

Aussie ISDA   full title *'The Australian Guide to AFMA/ISDA Standard Documentation'*, this provides standardised documentation for all Australian risk-management products as well as a guide for netting these transactions between counterparties. Aussie ISDA dates from the development, in the 1980s, of a standard master agreement for documenting risk-management products by the New York-based International Swaps and Derivatives Association (ISDA). In 1991, at the request of the Australian Financial Markets Association (AFMA), the legal firm Mallesons Stephen Jaques, with the cooperation of ISDA, prepared an Australian guide to facilitate the use of the ISDA master agreement in Australia. See **Australian Financial Markets Association, International Swaps and Derivatives Association, netting by master agreement**.

Australian Financial Markets Association   a national cooperative organisation created in 1986 in response to a need to streamline financial markets practices, to establish trading standards and conventions and to foster education and the development of Australian's financial sector along self-regulatory lines. *Abbrev.* **AFMA**.

automated pit trading the electronic after-hours trading system used at LIFFE-LTOM (the product of the merger between the London International Financial Futures Exchange and London Traded Options Market). *Abbrev.* **APT**.

average price/rate option an option whose settlement value is based on the difference between the strike and average price/rate of the underlying instrument on specified dates during the life of the option or some other nominated period which would also end with expiration of the option. Its premium is generally lower because the averaging process reduces volatility. Its theoretical value is also less than that of a corresponding conventional option. Also *Asian option*.

back-to-back in the futures market, back-to-back describes an equal number of bought and sold contracts held by one trader in one month. The term is also used to refer to offsetting loans, often made in one currency in one country against a loan in another currency in another country.

back-to-back loan a type of loan that first emerged in the 1960s to circumvent currency restrictions. See **parallel loan**.

backwardation a situation where prices are higher in the nearer delivery months than in the distant months. For example, if the SFE share-price index futures for a delivery in March stood at 1845.0 and for a June delivery at 1840.0 then the backwardation for three months to March would be 5 points. The opposite of backwardation is contango. Also *inverted market*. See **contango**.

barrier option an option whose payoff pattern and survival to expiration depend on not just the final price of the underlying asset but on whether the underlying asset sells at or beyond a barrier price during the life of the option:
- **down-and-in** barrier options carry the right to have an option but the option does not come into play unless the market falls to a predetermined level which triggers the option's existence;
- **up-and-in** options carry the right to have an option but the option does not come into play unless the market rises to a predetermined level which triggers the option's existence;

- **down-and-out** options carry the right to have an option but if the market falls to a predetermined level the options expire;
- **up-and-out** options carry the right to have an option but if the market rises to a predetermined level the options expire.

See **barrier price, knock-in, knock-out options**.

barrier price the instrike/outstrike price that activates or kills a barrier option. See **barrier option**.

basis the most common interpretation of basis is the difference between the cash market price and the futures market price. 'Basis trading' involves taking a view on the price differences between the cash market and the futures market.

basis point one-hundredth of 1 per cent. 100 basis points = 1 per cent, 10 basis points = 0.1 per cent; a bill yield that has moved from 8.20 per cent to 8.30 per cent has risen by 10 basis points. Basis point is the minimum fluctuation used for interest-rate products, eg, a basis point in the Sydney Futures Exchange's three-year bond futures contract is 0.01.

basis risk the possibility that an imperfectly matched hedge could produce a loss, eg, a hedger has taken offsetting positions in two related but not perfectly matched markets such as using bank-bill futures to hedge a position in two-year bonds.

basis swap an interest-rate swap carried out between two floating rates set against two different reference rates. The interest payments exchanged are calculated from two different floating-rate indexes, usually in $US, such indexes being the commercial paper or US prime rate, LIBOR, certificate of deposit rate or US treasury bill.

basis trading where a trader hopes to profit from changes in the relative prices of derivative and underlying instruments.

basket option an option on a basket of underlying stocks selected on the basis of their being suitably representative of certain industries, sectors or economies.

BBSW the Australian Financial Markets Association's bank-bill reference rate, published daily on AAP Reuters page BBSW.

bear floater   a structured security whose interest rate is periodically reset at a multiple of the floating reference index rate minus a fixed rate. The floating rate rises or falls by a multiple of the change in the floating-rate index to make a leveraged play on the upward direction of the short-end of the yield curve (rising trend in short-term interest rates). Bear floaters operate on assumptions about the degree and direction of anticipated changes to the yield curve; they work when the yield curve is inverse, ie, short rates are higher than longer-term rates. See **reverse floater**.

bear spread   an options market technique that aims to take advantage of a fall in price of a commodity or share. A trader would buy and sell options of the same class—sell lower strike price, buy higher strike price—for example, buy and sell call or put options on the same commodity or share, with the objective of benefiting from a fall in the price of the underlying commodity or share. A bear (or bull) spread can refer to a futures market position, as well as to an options technique, but is more commonly used with options. See **bull spread, option spread**.

bells and whistles   special add-on attractions that dress up an otherwise conventional investment or instrument to give it novelty. Bells and whistles can range from a cheque account with an interest-bearing sweep (retail product) to the more exotic capital market bonds and warrants. They are often used to improve the credit of securitised assets. The new twists are limited only by the imagination of the inventors—typically the Wall Street *wunderkinder*. See **rocket scientist, vanilla product**.

Bermuda option   like its namesake, the option falls somewhere between Europe and America—between a European option which can be exercised only at maturity and an American option which can be exercised at any point chosen by the holder. A Bermuda option usually can be exercised at any one of a number of points and this is stated in the option contract. Its premium value should fall between those of an American and European option, reflecting its midway position. Also *Atlantic option*.

best-buy option   a partial or full lookback call option. See **lookback option**.

beta factor   in futures and share trading, an estimate of the historical volatility (variability) of a commodity's price against a related composite index, for example, movements in the gold price against the precious metals index. If gold were to rise by 6 per cent and the index by 5 per cent, then gold's beta (β) would be 1.2, being the ratio of 6:5.

better-of-two-assets option   see **alternative option**.

bid-ask spread   the difference between the bid and offer prices. This can say a great deal about a market—about its liquidity, volume, depth and the enthusiasm or otherwise of its participants.

bilateral netting   an agreement between two parties under which they exchange only the net difference between what each owes the other. The chief objective is to reduce exposure to credit and settlement risk. See **netting by novation**.

bill option   in futures, an option over a bill futures contract. In banking, a line of credit which includes the option of using bills of exchange rather than cash, so that the loan can be liquidated by selling the bills. See **exchange-traded option, over-the-counter option**.

binary option   see **all-or-nothing option**.

Black–Scholes option pricing model   a device developed in 1973 by two US economists, Fischer Black and Myron Scholes, to help assess the value of option contracts. The model was influential in persuading the US Commodity Futures Trading Commission to allow options to be traded again (they had been banned since 1933) as it showed the potential of options for limiting risk. It has become the basic option-pricing formula. With the spread of computers, many companies have developed proprietary formulas of increasing complexity but most are in some way derived from the Black and Scholes model.

blended interest-rate swap   a combination of two or more interest-rate swaps where usually one starts spot and the other forward to produce payments calculated on a weighted average of rates.

BOATs   warrants whose value is tied to the yield between French OATs and German bunds, often referred to as the Maginot spread. See **Maginot spread, warrant**.

bond option   an option whose underlying security/instrument is a bond.

Boston option   a form of break forward, see **break forward.**

break forward   a type of option used mostly in the foreign-exchange markets to take full advantage of a move in the underlying asset beyond a predetermined level. The premium is paid at maturity. Also *Boston option, forward with optional exit (FOX)*.

bull spread   a technique involving the purchase and sale of the same class of options, although it can be used with conventional futures contracts. A bull spread would be the purchase and sale of call or put options (buy low strike, sell high in same class of options) on the same commodity, designed to benefit from a rise in market prices. See **bear spread, option spread**.

bunds   German government bonds.

butterfly spread   first used in fixed-interest markets and now in options to describe a spread or straddle position in the pattern of one-two-one; for example, a trader's position would be an agreement to sell one option contract maturing in, say, March, to buy two options maturing in June and to sell one option contract maturing in September. A butterfly spread—so called because when plotted on a profit expiry diagram it has the shape of a butterfly—enables a trader to change the mix of bought and sold securities in a way that does not alter the overall position, while exposures will differ depending on what happens to the yield curve (ie, to interest rates). It is a sophisticated trading strategy for managing risk; it has been popular with fund managers in the US and is expected to be used more frequently in other markets.

calendar roll   closing a futures or options position in one contract month and opening a position on the same side of the market in a more distant month.

calendar spread see **option spread**.

call   see **option**.

call option   see **option**.

call protection   provisions in a bond issue which stipulate a period during which the issuer cannot call an issue or must pay a premium over parity to retire the issue.

call provision   a term in a bond issue which gives the issuer the right to call the bond for redemption and/or refunding at certain prices and certain times.

callable swap   a swap agreement in which the fixed-rate receiver can terminate the swap on one or more specified dates before the stated maturity date. The potential early termination offers a chance to protect against large, adverse changes in interest rates; in the case of a fixed-rate receiver, against a large rise in rates which would cut the present value of cashflow from the swap. See **puttable swap**.

cap   a ceiling set on interest rates, offering a form of protection or insurance in that a borrower cannot pay more than the rate or price agreed under the cap contract. The cap holder gains protection from a rise in prices up to a specified level. A cap can be customised, ie, written by a financial institution for an individual client, or it can be in the form of a 'stripped' cap, one which is separated from a capital market transaction. Also *interest rate condom*. See **collar**.

cap and floor   see **interest-rate collar**.

caplet   an interim cap component in a multiperiod interest-rate cap agreement.

capped call   a long call position with a maximum payout.

capped lookback calls   a call option with a lookback strike and a maximum settlement price.

capped swap an interest-rate swap with a cap on the floating-rate payment.

caption an option to buy a cap.

cashflow swap a swap with irregular cashflows.

cash-futures swap see **exchange for physical**.

cash settlement settlement by payment of cash which is based on the difference between settlement price and a nominated benchmark or index. For example, settlement of futures contracts with a cash payment which reflects the difference between the settlement price and a chosen benchmark rather than by physical delivery of the instrument on which the contract is based, eg, bank-bill futures. Cash settlement can also refer to cash that is exchanged for securities delivered for settlement of a physical trade.

cash-settled option an option settled for an amount of cash equal to the difference, when the option is exercised, between the strike price and the spot price of the underlying instrument or asset. Traditionally, option contracts are settled by delivery of the underlying asset.

CARD *abbrev.* **certificate for amortising revolving debt**.

CATS *abbrev.* **certificate of accrual on treasury securities**.

certificate for amortising revolving debt a form of asset-backed security backed by a pool of car loans. *Abbrev.* **CARD**. See **asset-backed security**.

certificate of accrual on treasury securities zero-coupon bonds created by stripping US treasury securities of their coupon. *Abbrev.* **CATS**.

cherrypicking found in insolvency and bankruptcy proceedings, this refers to the practice of selecting contracts favourable to the bankrupt as those to be enforced and reneging on obligations to unsecured creditors. Netting and offset agreements used in swaps have been structured to prevent this.

churning trading for trading's sake, or to push up prices or generate commissions.

class (of options) options of the same type, eg a put or a call, based on the same underlying contracts or shares are termed as being in the same class.

clearing processing and settling a trade.

clearing house in futures trading, a clearing house is an organisation that maintains a continuous record of futures market trading. The clearing house has a separate identity from the futures exchange, although many clearing houses are exchange-owned. Clearing services for the Sydney Futures Exchange are provided by the Sydney Futures Exchange Clearing House (SFECH), a wholly-owned subsidiary of the SFE. See **International Commodities Clearing House, Sydney Futures Exchange Clearing House**.

close out in futures, foreign exchange and derivatives trading, to liquidate a position or fulfil an obligation by cancelling a contract (close-out by termination). Close-out by offset would involve, say, taking an equal and opposite position, for example, a trader who has bought a futures contract would close out, or exit the market, by selling a futures contract.

cocktail swap a complicated transaction based on several different types of swaps and involving more than two counterparties.

collar with a collar, a hedger buys a cap and sells a floor, using the proceeds from the sale of one to fund the cost of the other. The collar provides protection within a band—a cap sets a ceiling and a floor a minimum level. Collars are cheaper than outright caps because premium income is received on the sale of the floor. Also *cylinder, tunnel*. See **cap, floor**.

collar swap an interest-rate swap with a collar applying to the floating-rate payment stream.

collared FRN a floating-rate note with a collar.

combination option a package composed of several different options.

commodity option an option to buy or sell (call or put) a commodity such as oil or gold or a commodity futures contract at a specified strike price and within a specified period.

commodity swap   a swap where counterparties exchange cashflows based, at least on one side of the swap, on the price of a given commodity.

compound option   an option on an option, such as buying the right to buy a call option or the right to sell a call option. These are used mostly in fixed-interest and foreign-exchange markets where a trader is uncertain about buying the kind of risk protection provided by an option. The buyer of a compound option initially pays a reduced premium but may have to pay a second premium if the option is exercised.

condor   a complex option spread, similar to a butterfly spread but where all options have different strikes. See **butterfly spread**.

contango   a futures and commodity market expression to describe a situation where the spot prices are lower than those for transactions in forward months. See its opposite, **backwardation**.

convexity   a measure showing the sensitivity of the change in the price of a fixed-interest security in response to a change in interest rates. Convexity goes a stage beyond modified duration; it shows the difference between a bond's price change and its modified-duration-predicted price change (a linear relationship). See **modified duration**.

correlation   correlation refers to the historical statistical relationship between different markets, which can be used to take positions or cross-hedge or construct new instruments.

correlation risk   the risk that the price of something will change because of a change in the correlation. This can be offset by correlation hedging. See **correlation, delta**.

corridor   a combination of two caps, one bought by a borrower at a predetermined strike price and a second sold by a borrower at a higher strike which brings down the cost of the first.

cost of carry   the cost of funding a physical position which has to be priced into a transaction or arbitrage, eg, a physical/futures arbitrage where a physical position in, say, bank bills, has to be funded.

counterparty risk   the credit and performance risk in any financial transaction, such as a swap or foreign-exchange transaction. It is the risk that the party on the other side of the transaction might not meet its obligations. In futures trading, counterparty risk is with the clearing house.

country limit   the maximum amount a lender will provide to borrowers in a particular country, irrespective of the status or type of the borrower or of the currencies involved. Country limits form part of a lender's armoury of risk-management procedures.

country risk   the risk associated with dealing with another country, ie, a cross-border transaction, including legal, political, currency and settlement risks. Also *sovereign risk*.

coupon   the annual rate of interest promised to the bondholder. A 10 per cent coupon entitles the holder to receive $10 a year for each $100 invested, for the life of the bond, paid in two half-yearly instalments.

coupon swap   a conventional fixed-for-floating interest-rate swap.

covered call   a short call option covered by a long position in the underlying asset.

covered interest arbitrage   a form of riskless arbitrage, this technique involves exploiting the differential between interest rates and forward points which are out of line.

covered option   an option contract backed by ownership of the underlying physical. See **naked option**.

covered warrant   a warrant issue backed by the issuer's holding in the underlying.

covered writer   a call option writer owning the securities or commodities over which the option is written. See **naked option**.

crack spread   an oil refiner's operating margin—the difference between the prices of crude oil and those for refined products.

credit equivalent amount   the amount that results from translating a bank or investment bank's off-balance-sheet liabilities into the risk equivalent of loans, using Reserve Bank of Australia guidelines.

credit risk   the risk that an obligation will not be paid and a loss will result. This could stem from a counterparty defaulting on a payment due under a swap or other transaction, or from a decline in the market value of securities held. See **pre-settlement risk, settlement risk**.

credit risk premium   an additional amount included in a security's yield (or discounted price) which reflects what could be lost if the issuer were to default. A company rated AAA would not pay a risk premium when issuing securities; a company rated BB or less would.

credit spread   1. the difference between two securities' yields based solely on differences in credit quality; 2. an option spread which, when initiated, produces a net cash inflow to a trader or investor's account, eg, a bull call spread or a bear put spread. See **debit spread**.

credit watch   a warning issued by a credit-rating agency regarding a bank or company whose credit-rating it expects to downgrade—that organisation has been placed on 'credit watch'.

cross-currency basis swap   an interest-rate swap that calls for both counterparties being floating-rate payers in each's currency.

cross-currency cap   an option paying the holder the difference between the spread on two currency base rates and a strike spread.

cross-currency interest-rate swap   see **currency swap**.

cross-currency option   an option struck at an exchange rate between two currencies, generally with its premium in a third currency.

cross-currency settlement risk   a risk made famous in the 1970s by the failure of Germany's Herstatt Bank to pay what it owed in a foreign-exchange transaction after the other side had met its obligations. Cross-currency settlement risk is exacerbated by differences in time zones which often result in one party giving value (making its payment) before receiving value (receiving what it is due under the transaction from its counterparty). See **settlement risk**.

cross-currency swap   see **currency swap**.

cross hedging   a general term for hedging in different markets, say, offsetting the risk of one position by taking a position in another instrument or commodity whose features do not perfectly offset the position being hedged. For example, hedging a portfolio of semi-government securities with commonwealth bond futures. However, there is always the risk of mismatch.

cross rate   a rate calculated using the rates of two currencies against a third (usually the $US) to arrive at the relationship of the two currencies with each other. For example, if one $US were equal to 1.5 deutschmarks and 97 yen, then one deutschmark would equal 65 yen. In Australia, a quote of the $A against any currency except the $A/$US quote is referred to as a cross rate. In the US, a sterling/yen rate would be a cross rate.

currency coupon swap   a conventional swap in the sense that the interest rate in one currency is fixed and in the other is floating but different in that it involves different currencies.

currency option   an option that gives the holder, in exchange for a premium paid at the outset, the right but not the obligation to buy or sell a currency at a designated price over a stipulated period which ends at the expiration date of the option.

currency swap   a swap where the counterparties exchange equal principal amounts of two currencies at the spot exchange rate. During the life of the swap the counterparties exchange fixed or floating-rate interest payments in the swapped currencies and at maturity the principal amounts are again swapped at a predetermined rate of exchange (usually also the initial spot rate). Also **cross-currency swap, cross-currency and interest-rate swap, currency coupon swap**. See **FX swap**.

curve lock the base metals market term for an interest-rate swap.

custodian a bank or other financial institution holding securities on behalf of clients.

cylinder also *tunnel*. See **collar**.

day-trading buying into and selling out of the market within one day or one trading session. Similar to jobbing. Day-trading avoids holding an overnight position.

daylight exposure the risk that arises when related transactions are not settled simultaneously but at different times during the trading day, particularly relevant when dealing in different time zones.

debit spread an option spread which, when initiated, produces a net cash outflow from a trader's or investor's account, eg, a bull put spread or bear call spread. See **credit spread**.

debt-equity swap a method of refinancing where, in return for cancelling a debt, a debt holder receives an equity position.

debt instrument a bond or an IOU—an obligation to repay a fixed amount of money.

deferred coupon bond (note) a bond (note) paying no interest for a set period then paying interest at a higher rate than would otherwise be the case for the rest of its term.

deferred-interest bond a bond paying interest only from a set future date. A zero-coupon bond is the ultimate deferred-interest bond, paying all interest at maturity when the principal is also repaid.

deferred premium option an option whose premium is paid when it expires or is netted against any payoff. In all other respects the option is standard.

deferred payment swap a swap where some or all payments

are delayed for a specified time, usually for tax or accounting reasons.

deferred strike-price option   an option where the buyer can set the strike price at some date after the option is traded. See **exotic options**.

delayed start swap   a swap starting at a set future date.

deliverable   a financial instrument (eg, bank bill of exchange) or a commodity (eg, wool), traded on a futures exchange, that has been certified acceptable for delivery under an exchange's contract specifications. For example, to be accepted as deliverable bank bills (or substitute securities such as bank certificates of deposit) must mature within a specific range of dates.

delivery price   see **settlement price**.

delivery risk   see **settlement risk**.

delta   a measure of the proportional change between two items, this is used to track the change in an option price for a small change in the price of the underlying instrument. The delta (Δ) can vary between 0 and 1. If an option's delta is 0.5, a \$1 move in the price of the underlying asset will produce a 50-cent move in the option. See **delta hedging**.

delta hedging   a strategy used by option sellers to protect their exposure, ie, to be 'delta-neutral'. Delta hedging involves taking steps to offset price/rate risk by matching the market response of the underlying asset over a narrow range of price/rate movements. (Option buyers do not need to worry about delta hedging because their potential loss is limited to the outlay of an initial premium.) To structure a delta hedge, an option seller takes into account changes in the spot price, the time to expiry and the difference between the strike and spot prices. The more an option is in-the-money the greater is the amount of delta hedging. A deep in-the-money option has a delta of close to 1, or even 1, because it is likely to be exercised; a deep out-of-the money option would be close to or at zero because the option has very little intrinsic value. See **delta variable, gamma hedge**.

delta-neutral   positions described as delta-neutral would have offsetting positive and negative deltas to remove or neutralise the response to small market movements.

delta variable   this measures the likelihood of an option being exercised and so determines how much an option writer should hedge to be delta-neutral, ie, covered. See **delta, delta hedging**.

derivative products   contracts or instruments whose value stems from that of some underlying asset, such as commodities, equities or currencies, or from an index such as the stock-exchange index, or from an indicator such as an interest rate. Derivative products include swaps, forwards, futures, options (puts and calls), swaptions, caps, floors and collars. The list is constantly evolving. See **exotic options**.

derivatives book-runner   a bank or investment bank managing and trading a portfolio of swaps, options and other derivative products. See **derivative products**.

derivatives house   a bank, investment bank or brokerage firm specialising in structuring and trading swaps, options and other derivative products. See **derivative products**.

detachable warrant   a warrant once issued with a bond or other security but which has been separated and traded independently. Common in the euromarkets.

diagonal spread see **option spread**.

diff swap   see **rate differential swap**.

digital option   also *binary option*. See **all-or-nothing option**.

discount   a reduction in price either from a previous price or from face value. See **premium**.

discount swap   a swap using the coupon of a discount bond or bill as the fixed-rate or floating-rate payment. See **non-par swap**.

dual-coupon swap   a fixed-for-floating interest-rate swap which includes a call option giving one party the right to have periodic settlements made in another currency if exchange rates move against the base currency used in the swap.

dual-currency bond   a fixed-interest security paying a coupon in a base currency (generally the currency of the investor) while the principal is in another (non-base) currency (usually the currency of the issuer). A dual-currency bond can be modified in a number of ways. See **indexed currency option notes (ICONs), reverse dual-currency bond**.

dual-currency option   an option settled in either of two currencies at the choice of the option-holder.

dual-currency swap   a swap used to hedge the issue of a dual-currency bond, it is typically used by a financial intermediary to take on the elements of a dual-currency bond that are not wanted by the issuer.

dual trading   trading for individual/house and customer accounts at the same time. This can raise the issue of conflict of interest.

duration   see **Macaulay duration, modified duration**.

duration gap   the difference between the maturity of a portfolio of assets and that of its offsetting liabilities.

duration matching   see **portfolio immunisation**.

dynamic hedging   portfolio insurance or risk management which increases or reduces the underlying position to maximise gains and minimise losses. It calls for constant re-assessing and re-adjusting of the hedge and is only possible in deep and liquid markets where transaction costs will not consume any benefits derived from hedging. See **delta hedge, portfolio insurance**.

earnings at risk   see **value at risk**.

EFP   *abbrev.* **exchange for physical**.

embedded option   an option that forms an inseparable element of another instrument, usually in the form of an option enabling a party to exit ahead of schedule from an arrangement, eg, a provision in a corporate bond issue whereby the issuer can repay the lender ahead of the maturity date of the bond.

equity warrant   see **warrant**.

escalating swap   see **accreting principal swap**.

eurobond   issued since the 1960s, eurobonds are used by top-credit borrowers, such as banks and large international companies, to raise medium to long-term fixed-interest funds. The investment bank Morgan Guaranty defined the eurobond as 'a bond underwritten by an international syndicate and sold in countries other than the country of the currency in which the issue is denominated'.

euromarkets   the markets for eurobonds and eurocurrencies—ie, currencies and securities held outside their country of origin. In this context, *euro-* signifies external. Euromarkets date from 1957 when non-US banks holding $US deposits began to reinvest them in Europe instead of in the US. The UK banks played a major role in lending $US to European banks, companies and individuals. Euromarkets are also said to have been encouraged by the cold war between the US and the then Soviet Union. The Soviet Union was anxious about holding dollars in the US, so it placed them with the UK's Midland Bank, which then lent them to customers. At the time, US banks were operating under restrictions which held their deposit rates substantially lower than those of their European counterparts, so that European banks' higher rates were able to attract $US deposits. London was the first euromarket centre and is still the largest. See **eurobond**.

European option   a put or call option that cannot be exercised before its expiry date. See **American option, over-the-counter options**.

exchange for physical   a transaction in which a physical commodity or financial instrument, eg, a government bond or interest-rate swap is traded and an offsetting futures hedge transaction is simultaneously undertaken. EFPs are not executed on the floor of the Sydney Futures Exchange but are traded either directly between the two parties concerned or through a fixed-interest broker. The appeal of EFPs is that the parties to the trade are free to negotiate the futures price. As a result, fund managers and other institutional investors often use EFPs to switch or modify exposures between the cash and futures markets. *Abbrev.* **EFP.**

exchange-traded option an option traded on a recognised exchange, with contract specifications set by the exchange and traders margined. See **option**.

exempt market a market relieved of most of the provisions of Chapter 7 or Chapter 8 of the Corporations Law—which regulates securities and futures trading—because transactions are carried out between professionals.

exercise (of an option) converting an option into its underlying futures contract or into the shares covered by the option, by paying the predetermined amount.

exercise price see **strike price**.

exotic options options with unusual features, be that an unusual underlying asset or intrument or method of calculating the strike price or payout. Examples include **barrier options, dual currency options, deferred strike-price options, lookback options**. Also *non-standard option*.

expiry date the date on which an option expires (matures). An option buyer wishing to exercise the option must do so either on or before expiry date.

extrinsic value see **time value**.

fairway option devised by Citibank Ltd, a fairway option is similar to a collar but links two different variables, eg, the gold price and a currency. A borrower/client sells a cap and sells a floor, taking a view that one variable (the one moving in the 'fairway') will always stay within the band between the cap and the floor (the fairway). It is a risky trade, being a play on volatility.

financial engineering see **zaitek**.

financial futures instruments with which to hedge or protect against movements in interest rates, share prices and currencies. They have thrived since the mid-1970s as investors, traders and speculators seized on a new method to protect themselves against, or make money out of, increasingly volatile interest rates and exchange rates. Financial futures began in the US in the early 1970s; currency futures started trading in 1972 in Chicago and interest rate futures followed in 1976. The Sydney Futures Exchange was the first outside the US to move into financial futures, with the launch of the bank bill contract in October 1979. Since then financial futures trading in Australia has expanded to include share-price index futures and government bond futures. Other regional financial centres have embraced financial futures. See **futures markets**.

firm price (quote)   a price (quote) at which a trader is prepared to trade at a given time. A trader might qualify a quote by saying: 'My price is firm for 10 minutes.' Opposite of **indicative price (quote)**.

fixed-fixed currency swap   a currency swap where each side is a fixed-rate payer in its currency, and fixed-interest payments in one currency are swapped for fixed-interest payments in another.

fixed-floating-rate swap   the basic 'vanilla' interest-rate swap involving an exchange of fixed-rate payments for floating-rate payments in the same currency.

fixed-rate payer   a party in an interest-rate swap making a series of identical payments, eg, on the coupon of a fixed-interest instrument such as a bond, and receiving the floating rate. Also **floating-rate receiver**.

fixed-rate receiver   the party receiving a fixed rate and paying floating under a swap. See **fixed-rate payer**.

flat forward   see **par forward**.

floating-floating swap   see **basis swap**.

floating-rate note   a form of security, popular in the euromarkets and adopted elsewhere, issued for three years or longer and carrying a variable interest rate which is adjusted regularly (at one-to-six-monthly intervals—whatever preferred by the issuer) by a margin against a benchmark rate such as LIBOR. Increased volatility in interest rates helped the popularity of

FRNs as borrowers and lenders became reluctant to commit funds for a fixed period at a fixed rate. *Abbrev.*: **FRN**. See **LIBOR**.

floating-rate payer   a party in an interest-rate swap making a series of variable interest-rate payments. These are generally set with reference to an index or benchmark rate specified in the swap contract. Also **fixed-rate receiver**.

floating-rate receiver   the party receiving a floating rate and paying fixed under a swap agreement. See **fixed-rate payer, floating-rate payer**.

floor   a contract that protects the holder against a fall in prices beyond a specified level.

floortion   an option on a floor, giving the holder the right to buy a floor at a certain strike price for a specified premium on or before the date the floortion expires.

force majeure clause   a provision in a contract that releases the parties from their obligations in the event of circumstances— war, flood or other natural disaster beyond anyone's control—that block completion of the deal or contract.

forward   a future commitment whose terms are established now. A contract under which one side will buy and the other sell a specific asset at a set price on a given future date.

forward break   see **break forward**.

forward currency swap   a currency swap starting on a forward (future) date. Terms are agreed in advance. Such a swap can be used to hedge or establish a level of interest rates or exchange rates.

forward market   a market where traders and speculators can take out contracts for purchases or sales of commodities at a future date, in specified volumes and at specified prices. Futures trading is an example of a forward market. See **forward rate, spot, swaps**.

forward margin   the margin (points) added to the spot rate of exchange to arrive at a forward rate. The forward margin reflects the differential in interest rates between the two currencies concerned. See chapter 3.

forward rate   the price for a commodity, such as a foreign currency, for delivery some time more than two business days hence. Forward rates in currencies comprise the spot rate plus or minus a forward margin. See forward margin.

forward-rate agreement   an agreement between two parties seeking to protect themselves against a future interest-rate movement in a particular currency, for a specified period and at an agreed contract rate. Settlement is effected between the two parties for the difference between the contract rate and the interest settlement rate. *Abbrev*. **FRA**.

forward swap   a swap agreement arranged to start from a future date.

forward with optional exit   a form of break forward. *Abbrev*. **FOX**. See **break forward**.

FOX   *abbrev*. **forward with optional exit**.

fraption   an option on a forward-rate agreement.

fungible   when one unit of a commodity is equal to any other similar unit, eg, grains of wheat or corn, these are termed fungible. One can be substituted for the other with no change in value. Dollar coins of the same amount (unless a rare collector's item) are fungible, but bills of exchange and coins of different values are not. In futures markets fungible contracts are those that can be opened in one market and closed in another, eg, eurodollar contracts traded on Simex and the IMM.

futures contract   an agreement to buy or sell a standard quantity of a commodity—such as gold, $US or bank bills of exchange—on a specific future date at an agreed price determined at the time the contract is traded on the futures exchange. It is a binding contract, enforceable at law. Futures contracts are traded by open outcry on most futures exchanges' trading floor; an exception is the New Zealand Futures and Options Exchange, which has always used screen trading. The computer age is bringing the prospect of screen trading to other exchanges. See clearing house, contract, futures markets, Sydney Futures Exchange Clearing House, Sydney Computerised Overnight Market.

futures markets Futures markets have existed for centuries but evolved in their present form in the US in the nineteenth century. Chicago, in the midst of the grain and farming belt, emerged as the home of futures trading. The Chicago Board of Trade, established in 1850, focused on grain; the Chicago Mercantile Exchange began a few years later, dealing in butter and eggs. The exchanges provided traders with the means to take out protection against vagaries in the prices of their commodities. The exchanges also provided speculators with a new outlet. See **Sydney Futures Exchange**.

FX swap a purchase of one currency against another at an initial date and an agreement to reverse that transaction at a future date and at a specified rate.

gamma a measure of the rate of change in delta in response to changes in the price of the underlying asset or instrument, represented by the Greek letter γ. See **delta**.

gamma hedge this entails initiating option positions to reduce the risk of change to an options portfolio's delta in response to changes in the underlying over a narrow range of price movements.

gamma neutral positions described as gamma neutral would have offsetting positive and negative gammas to reduce the variations in a portfolio's delta in response to market movements.

gensaki rate the repurchase rate on Japanese government bonds.

good delivery bar a gold bar which meets the requirements of the London Bullion Markets Association. Its gold content is between 350 and 430 troy ounces and it must carry the stamp of an approved refiner.

grantor a seller (in the context of option trading). See **option**.

Group of Thirty A private, independent, Washington DC-based international organisation whose charter is to raise awareness and understanding of major international economic and financial issues. Its members include representatives of central banks, international banks and securities houses, and academia. The Group of Thirty (G30) is possibly best known for its comprehensive report and recommendations on the use of derivatives, released in 1993.

Hammersmith & Fulham   a London borough which gained a high profile in the late 1980s when it became very active in sterling swaps to an extent that suggested speculation rather than hedging. The speculation was unsuccessful and ultimately deemed *ultra vires*—outside the borough's legal scope of activities—by the UK high court. See chapter 9.

harmless warrant   also *wedding warrant*. See **warrant**.

heaven and hell bond   a type of dual-currency bond where the redemption rate of the principal amount is based on the change in the spot exchange rate from the time the bond is issued to its maturity.

hedge fund   a pool of assets managed actively, even aggressively, on behalf of the owners of the assets, generally private high-net-worth individuals. The pool can include a range of financial instruments and securities. Fund managers are generally paid a percentage of the profits as a fee.

hedging   taking steps to protect against, or at least reduce, a risk; a form of insurance. The term is common in futures and foreign-exchange markets where traders use facilities available to protect themselves against future price or exchange rate variations. If someone bulk buys scotch whisky ahead of the budget in anticipation of a price rise in the budget, then he or she is hedging (provided the whisky is drunk—if it were bought to be onsold, then the buyer is speculating).

Herstatt Risk   see **cross-currency settlement risk**.

hindsight option   a type of *lookback option*, this gives the holder the right, while the option is valid, to retrospectively buy a currency at its lowest level (with a call option) or sell at its peak (with a put).

historic volatility   see **volatility**.

horizontal spread   see **option spread**.

hybrid debt   a debt instrument that combines the features of debt and equity. Also *hybrid security*.

ICCH   abbrev. **International Commodities Clearing House**.

ICONs   *abbrev.* **indexed currency option notes**.

implied volatility   see **volatility**.

in-arrears swap   a conventional interest-rate swap structure with one difference—the floating rate is set retrospectively. It is calculated at the end of a specified reset period, using a reference rate. Also *arrears swap, reset swap*.

in the money   a term used to describe an option that can be exercised at a profit. The option contract's current market price is higher than the strike price of a call option or lower than the strike price of a put option. A call option on a financial instrument or commodity would be in the money at a strike price of 50 if the underlying instrument or commodity were selling for 51 or more; a put option at a strike price of 50 would be in the money if the instrument or commodity were selling at 49 or less. See **at the money, instrinsic value, out of the money**.

index arbitrage   an investment or trading strategy which attempts to maximise returns by shifting between long and short market positions and buying and selling share-price index futures contracts. See **program trading**.

index-linked bonds/notes   securities whose principal and/or interest payments are linked to the performance of a particular index, such as a sharemarket index.

index participations   introduced in 1989 by the Philadelphia Stock Exchange and the American Stock Exchange, these were structured to offer small investors a low-cost entry to a trading portfolio. A federal court judged index participations to be futures contracts and so not tradeable on securities exchanges. The instruments were delisted. See **Low Exercise Price Option**.

index warrants   put and call options on an index or index futures contract with more than one year to maturity, issued by companies or sovereign borrowers.

indexed currency option notes   a euronote issue that includes a currency option. First seen in 1985, the notes are serviced in one currency while the payment of the principal is indexed to another and converted at the exchange rate prevailing when the notes mature. *Abbrev.* **ICONs.**

indicative price (quote)   bid or offer price provided by way of information rather than as the level at which a trader is willing to trade. Indicative prices (quotes) enable a customer to plan a transaction but the transaction does not proceed until firm prices are provided. See **firm price (quote)**.

Individual Share Futures   share futures contracts traded on the Sydney Futures Exchange, based on individual stocks listed on the Australian Stock Exchange. Buying a share futures contract gives a financial exposure to (usually) the financial equivalent of 1000 shares in the underlying company. Initial margins are less than 5 per cent of the underlying contract so buyers of individual share futures gain a leveraged exposure to the shares. *Abbrev.* **ISF.**

initial margin (deposit)   the amount paid by a trader in the futures and options markets to cover against losses that might be incurred because of movements in the price of the instruments or commodities traded. It is a cash buffer set by the clearing house. The deposit level can vary, depending on the price volatility in the contract concerned, and represents an estimate of the maximum likely one-day price movement in the contract. If interest rates or gold were moving rapidly every day the deposit margin would be increased to take account of the uncertainty. See **margin call**.

intercommodity spread   where a trader buys or sells an instrument, eg, a 90-day bank-bill futures contract, and simultaneously sells or buys another related instrument, eg, a three-year bond futures contract. As with an intermonth spread, the rationale behind the strategy is to profit from the changing price differential between the two instruments. Transactions involving interest-rate instruments are commonly traded to take advantage of changes in the shape of the yield curve. See **intermonth spread**.

interest-rate collar   a combination of an interest-rate cap and an interest-rate floor. The buyer of a collar buys a cap option to limit the maximum interest rate to be paid and sells a floor option to partially offset the premium paid for the cap. A collar restricts interest-rate payments to a band between the strike prices of the cap and floor options. See **zero-cost collar**.

interest-rate condom   see **cap**.

interest-rate differential   the difference between the interest rates paid on debt instruments, eg, the interest-rate differential (spread) between $US bonds yielding 9 per cent and Swiss franc bonds yielding 4 per cent is 5 percentage points.

interest-rate futures   futures contracts based on financial instruments such as bank bills of exchange or government bonds which allow traders and investors to take out protection against future movements in interest rates. See **financial futures**, **futures markets**.

interest-rate option   see **bond option**.

interest-rate risk   exposure to loss resulting from a change in interest rates. Hedging strategies are designed to minimise, possibly eliminate, interest-rate risk.

interest-rate swap   a basic fixed-rate for floating-rate swap organised in one currency, with interest-rate flows paid in arrears and settled on a net cash basis.

interest-rate swap option   another variation on the interest-rate swap, this enables a borrower to take an option to enter into a future interest-rate swap at an agreed rate. Also known as *swaptions*.

intermonth spread   a strategy similar to a calendar or horizontal spread but used with futures contracts as well as in options trading. It involves buying one month of a contract and selling a different month of the same contract, for example buying the December three-year bond futures contract and at the same time selling the March three-year bond contract, with the aim of making a profit from the change in the price differential between the two contract months. See **option spread**, **straddle**.

International Securities Markets Association based in Zurich, Switzerland, ISMA was founded in 1969 as the Association of International Bond Dealers. Its name was changed in 1992. As world regulator for the eurobond markets, ISMA's statutes, by-laws, rules and recommendations form the core of the regulatory framework of the international securities markets. *Abbrev.* **ISMA.**

International Swaps and Derivatives Association a US-based international trade association which sets standard documentation and helps markets work with regulators. *Abbrev.* **ISDA.**

International Commodities Clearing House ICCH has provided clearing and guaranteeing services for London futures markets since 1888, when it was established as The London Products Clearing House. Its name was changed in 1973. ICCH's identity is quite separate from that of the exchange; its main role is to provide a registration service for all contracts and to guarantee the performance of each contract to its members. *Abbrev.* **ICCH.** See **Sydney Futures Exchange Clearing House**.

intrinsic value in the context of options trading, the amount by which an option is in the money. In the case of a call option, it is the amount by which the market price of, say, a share is above the strike price of the option covering it, so that exercising the option over the share is a better buy than buying the share outright. See **time value**.

inverse floater see **reverse floater**.

ISDA *abbrev.* **International Swaps and Derivatives Association**.

ISF *abbrev.* **Individual Share Futures**.

ISMA *abbrev.* **International Securities Markets Association**.

inverted market see **backwardation**.

inverted yield curve see **yield curve**.

investment grade   a bond or note rated at least BBB by Standard & Poor's or a similar credit-rating agency.

kilo bar   a one-kilogram bar of gold, a standard specification in gold trading, popular with jewellers.

knock-in option   down-and-in or up-and-in barrier options that do not exist until a predetermined price is triggered in the underlying asset or instrument. See **barrier options**.

knock-out option   down-and-out or up-and-out puts and calls that expire if a predetermined price level in the underlying asset or instrument is triggered. See **barrier options**.

kurtosis   the degree to which a statistical distribution is sharply peaked at its centre.

LBO   *abbrev.* **leveraged buy-out**.

leg in the air   a futures market situation where a trader is looking to complete a straddle; the trader may take a view on market movements that suggests doing one leg of the straddle first and completing the second leg later the same day. Both legs of the straddle have to be executed within one day to qualify as a straddle. Traders talk of 'lifting a leg' which indicates liquidating one leg of an existing straddle. Those who get caught with a 'leg in the air' or 'leg up' have to get out of it as best they can. See **straddle**.

legal right of set-off   see **netting**.

legal risk   in the context of financial risk management a vital legal risk relates to capacity or *ultra vires*, being the risk that a counterparty is not legally able to enter into a contract. Another legal risk relates to regulatory risk, ie, that a transaction could conflict with a regulator's policy or, more generally, that legislation might change during the life of a financial contract. See **Hammersmith & Fulham**.

LEPO   *abbrev.* **Low Exercise Price Option**.

leverage   financial power; the potential to make profits far in excess of the outlay required to gain entry to an investment or position. For example, futures contracts offer huge leverage because, for an initial margin payment, an investor can build up and control a large parcel of bonds or shares. Options also offer leverage.

leveraged buy-out   a technique used to take control of a company, using debt rather than equity. *Abbrev.*: **LBO**. See **MBO**.

LIBOR   see **London Inter Bank Offered Rate**.

lifting a leg   see **leg in the air**.

liquidity   the capacity to be converted easily and with minimum loss into cash. A liquid market is one in which there is enough activity to satisfy both buyers and sellers.

local   in futures markets, a person who trades on the futures exchange on his or her own personal account, not as a broker. Often known as a scalper.

loco   a term used in commodity markets, meaning 'at' (from the Latin *locus*, place). A trader would talk of gold traded 'loco London' meaning gold held in London and priced for delivery in London; gold can also be quoted 'loco Tokyo or loco Zurich'.

London Inter Bank Offered Rate   the rate used as a benchmark in eurodollar lending, it is the rate of interest charged by the major London banks on call money loans made among themselves. Borrowers are generally charged a margin over (rarely under) LIBOR, with the margin or spread varying in line with the borrower's credit-standing. *Abbrev.* **LIBOR**.

long position   long denotes an asset position, ie, a trader has bought more of a commodity than he or she has sold. Someone with a long position benefits from a rising (bull) market. See **short position**.

long the basis   a long position in the cash market and a short position in a future or forward market. See **basis, short the basis**.

long-dated forward   a forward contract whose settlement date is more than one year away.

long-dated option   an option with an exercise date more than one year hence.

lookback option   an option giving the buyer the retrospective right to buy or sell the underlying asset at its lowest or highest level within the period specified under the lookback agreement. Also **hindsight currency option**.

lookforward option   an option giving the buyer the future right to the difference between the strike price at the start of a specified period and its peak (if a call) or trough (if a put) over that period.

Low Exercise Price Options   devised by the Australian Stock Exchange in 1994, a form of deep in-the-money options whose risk profile is similar to that of a futures contract. The buyer is margined and, for a low entry price, gains control over a large parcel of shares. *Abbrev*. **LEPO**.

LTFX   a long-term, ie, beyond twelve-month, forward foreign-exchange contract.

Macaulay duration   A market-value, weighted measure of the time to maturity of a security. With fixed-interest securities, or any known set of cashflows, it is the sum of the time to each cashflow (eg, coupon payment) weighted by the ratio of the market value of each cashflow to the total market value of the security. The concept was devised in the US in 1938 by Frederick Macaulay, as a measure to capture the characteristics of bonds rather than merely classifying them by maturity.

Maginot spread   the difference between the yields on German *bunds* (bonds) and French *OATs* (*obligations assimilables du Trésor, government bonds*).

management buy-out   a change of ownership in a company where those running the business become the major shareholders. Most management buy-outs involve a degree of leverage. *Abbrev*. **MBO**. See **leveraged buy-out**.

margin account   a loan facility established for a futures trader by his or her futures broker or bank, to be drawn on to meet margin calls.

margin call   a request for funds to cover an unfavourable movement in price in the futures and options markets. Margin calls are made by the clearing house on its members, who in turn call clients. If a client fails to meet a margin call, the clearing member can close out that client's position in the marketplace, and the client has to carry any loss incurred. A margin call has two stages: the clearing house issues a statement to the clearing member early in the morning; the clearing member then contacts the clients concerned. It is the clearing member who is liable to the clearing house for the funds demanded—the clearing house recognises only the obligations of the member, not those of the client. Margin call money must be lodged by a specified time, otherwise the member is in default. Also *variation margin*. See **initial margin**.

margin spread concession a reduced margin, calculated by the Sydney Futures Exchange Clearing House, for offsetting positions in pairs of related contracts, eg, for a trader short (has sold) three-year bond futures and long (has bought) 10–year bond futures, or one who is long BHP Individual Share Futures and short share-price index futures.

mark to market to value assets at current market prices, as distinct from historical cost; a method of calculating gains or losses using closing or settlement prices at the end of the day. All futures contracts are marked to market by the clearing house to determine margin calls. Marking a portfolio of derivatives to market shows the value of the portfolio and the market risk attached to it, and enables decisions about what hedging strategy should be adopted. The Group of Thirty report recommended that derivatives dealers mark their portfolios to market at least daily. See **Group of Thirty**.

market maker a bank or financial institution prepared to quote buy-and-sell prices (two-way prices) in securities, financial instruments or derivatives.

market-if-touched order an order to buy or sell if and when the market price reaches a specified level. Once the specified price level is reached, it becomes a market order and is carried out. For example, a trader might place a market-if-touched order to buy bank-accepted bills at 93.00 when the bills are selling for 93.20; once the price drops to 93.00 the trade will be executed on the buyer's behalf as a market order. Used widely in futures trading. It is often used to initiate an order, perhaps to take advantage of a signal generated by technical analysis. Also called a *board order* (and *market watch* in OTC markets). *Abbrev.* **MIT**. See **stop order**.

market on close   an order to buy or to sell at the market price at the close of the day's trading. *Abbrev.* **MOC**.

market order   an instruction to buy or sell a commodity or share at the current market price. Also **at market order**.

market risk   the possibility that future earnings could be adversely affected by a change in market prices caused by movements in interest rates or exchange rates.

Matilda bonds   global bonds, first sold in 1991, denominated in $A and issued by supranationals such as the European Investment Bank and the Swedish Export Credit Corporation.

maturity mismatch risk   the risk in a cross hedge that because the long and short positions have different maturities the exposures will not be perfectly offset.

MBO   *abbrev.* **management buy-out**.

mini-max floater   a floating-rate note with an embedded collar, providing a return in a specified band. Used in the euromarkets.

mismatch risk   the market risk created if a hedge does not exactly cover an exposure.

MIT   *abbrev.* **market-if-touched order**.

MOC   *abbrev.* **market on close**.

modified duration   this measures the proportional change in the value of an instrument that results from a change in interest rates, ie, it shows a security's sensitivity to interest rates.

Monte Carlo simulation   a method of random sampling to achieve numerical solutions to mathematical problems.

mortgage-backed securities   instruments representing an interest in a pool of mortgages, issued in the US by the Federal

National Mortgage Association (Fannie Mae) and the Government National Mortgage Association (Ginnie Mae). A major issuer in Australia has been FANMAC; large issuers include Citibank and PUMA, a 100% subsidiary of Macquarie Bank Ltd.

multilateral netting   offsetting of receivables and payables among three or more parties to a transaction, with each making payments to an agent or clearing house for net obligations due to others or receiving net payments due from others. The process reduces credit and settlement risk. See **netting**.

mutual offset   the ability to buy or sell in one market and close out the position in the same commodity or contract in another market; eg, to trade the eurodollar contract on the Singapore International Monetary Exchange (Simex) and close it out on the Chicago Mercantile Exchange (CME).

naked option   an option whose writer has not hedged—eg, a writer of call options over shares who has sold the right to buy the underlying shares but who does not own them, or the writer of a put option over shares who has sold the right to sell the shares (to the writer); if the holder chooses to exercise the option the uncovered writer will be obliged to buy the shares at an exercise price which will be a higher-than-market price (otherwise the holder of the option would not exercise). Naked options are high-risk and can involve large losses for a writer. See chapters 5 and 6.

natural hedge   a position which establishes assets or borrowings in a currency that provides an offset to expected cashflows; for example, an Australian-based company with operations in Germany which provide a natural hedge against its deutschmark borrowings.

negative carry   where the cost of funds borrowed to finance an investment outweighs the yield on the assets. Borrowing at 10 per cent to invest in bonds yielding 8 per cent would produce a negative carry but a trader would expect the negative carry to be outweighed by a capital gain or trading/arbitrage profit. See **positive carry**.

negative mark-to-market   a paper loss. Bonds bought at a yield of 9 per cent when the market is 11 per cent are showing a negative mark-to-market of 2 per cent (but still earning 9 per cent).

negative straddle   see **straddle**.

netting   offsetting payables against receivables so that settlement is effected by a cheque for the net amount. This reduces counterparty credit exposure.

netting by novation   replacing all agreements between two parties with a single agreement and single net payment stream.

netting by master agreement   an umbrella contract under which all transactions executed between parties to the agreement are automatically netted, ie, amounts due and owing are offset. For example, Party A and Party B are two of the several signatories to a master agreement covering, among other transactions, swaps. Under a swap, Party A owes Party B $200 but Party B owes Party A $300 so a net cheque for the difference of $100 is paid, rather than the parties exchanging cheques for the full amounts. See **Aussie ISDA**.

non-par swap   a swap where one or both of the securities underlying the swap sells at a discount or premium, ie, at a non-market rate, and compensation is usually made for this. Also *off-market swap*. See **discount swap**.

non-standard option   see **exotic options**.

notional principal   the amount in a swap which forms the basis for calculating payment streams. With interest-rate swaps the principal amount is not exchanged at the outset or at maturity.

novation   generally, assigning or replacing one or a series of contracts with new contracts, often with a third party replacing one of the originals. Also a futures market term to describe the clearing-house process which allows one party's open position obligation to another to be switched to a new entrant as one of the initial (two) parties to the contract withdraws. Novation results in the clearing house being the central counterparty to all transactions on the futures exchange. See **open position**.

OATs   abbrev. *obligations assimilables du Trésor*.

obligations assimilables du Trésor   French government bonds, the basis of the French bond futures and options contracts. *Abbrev.* **OATs**.

off-balance-sheet instrument   an instrument or contract, such as a swap or option, that changes a company's risk profile but which appears in the notes to the accounts and not as an asset or a liability in the balance sheet.

off-market swap   see **non-par swap**.

oil-price derivatives   risk-management products whose underlying instrument is an oil index.

open interest   the number of open contracts in a futures market or in a particular class of options. The Australian convention is to include in the daily figures published by the SFE all unmatched bought contracts and all unmatched sold contracts; the convention elsewhere is to show one side only of transactions.

open position   a futures contract which has been bought or sold and not offset by an opposite position in the same delivery month. More generally, it is the difference between total purchases and total sales, ie, exposure to interest-rate or currency risk.

option   a contract which gives the holder, in return for paying a premium to the option seller, the right to buy or sell a financial instrument or commodity during a given period. Option trading is used in the futures and share markets and a significant volume of option trading takes place over-the-counter (OTC), ie, not on an exchange. Financial futures options were introduced on the Sydney Futures Exchange in 1982 and were the first such options in the world. Futures options offer buyers a useful method of limiting risk: if the option is not exercised the option taker (buyer) is limited in outlay to the cost of the premium on the option, plus brokerage. Options can be either *call options*, which give the option holder, in return for paying a premium, the right to buy from the grantor of the option at the strike price, or *put options* which give the option holder, in return for paying a premium, the right to sell to the grantor of the option at the strike price. See **American option, Asian option, European option, exchange-traded option, futures markets, option spread, option straddle, over-the-counter options, strike price**.

option on a floor   see **floortion**.

option on a swap   see **swaption**.

option spread   a strategy used by an options trader hoping to gain from the difference between the prices of two options, ie, simultaneously buying one option and selling another of the same type on the same futures contract, security or index. If the number of options bought is not the same as the number sold then a *ratio option* has been initiated. There are several types of option spreads (which also apply to futures and physical markets): *horizontal* or *calendar spread* is the simultaneous buying and selling of the same class of options, at the same strike price but at different premiums and with different expiry dates; a *vertical spread* is the simultaneous buying and selling of the same class of options, at different strike prices but with the same expiry date; a *diagonal spread* is a combination of vertical and calendar spreads in which the trader buys and sells the same class of options at different strike prices and with different expiry dates. See **bear spread, bull spread**.

option straddle   a strategy which uses both a put and call option: the trader who buys a straddle (buys a put and a call) will make money no matter which way the market moves—provided that the size of the movement is sufficient to cover the cost of the two premiums paid. Buyers of straddles are therefore hoping for large price movements to occur while sellers of straddles (sellers of a put and a call) are hoping for prices to remain largely unchanged.

option writer   a seller of an option.

out of the money   a term used to describe an option that cannot be exercised at a profit. An out-of-the-money option is a call option whose strike price is higher than the current market level, or a put option whose strike price is below market. A call option on December bonds at 100 would be out of the money if December bonds were 99 or less; a put option would be out of the money if they were at 101 or more. An out-of-the-money option has no intrinsic value but does have some time value, except at expiry. See **at the money, in the money, time value**.

over-the-counter option   an option that can be tailored to individual clients' needs. The client arranges the option with his or her bank or merchant bank, instead of buying an 'off-the-peg' model such as an exchange-traded option, so that details such as amount, maturity and prices are arranged between client and bank. Over-the-counter (OTC) options cannot be traded but they can be sold back to the bank or merchant bank which initiated the product. These options are a useful hedging device (relying on a degree of trust between client and the bank/merchant bank) and, like exchange-traded options, involve the payment of a premium. See **exchange-traded option, option**.

par forward   a facility favoured by gold producers which evens out the price curve or income stream (normally in contango in the gold market) to provide a constant price for the life of the transaction. This produces steady cashflow and also brings forward some income. A par forward in foreign exchange markets is a series of contracts with the same forward rate applying to all forward commitments to produce an even set of foreign-currency cashflows. Also *flat forward*. See **contango** and chapter 7.

parallel loan   the forerunner of a swap; a method of raising capital in a foreign country to finance assets there without a cross-border movement of capital. For example, a $US loan would be made to an Australian company to finance its factory in the US; at the same time the US party which made the loan would borrow $A in Australia from the Australian company's parent to finance a project in Australia. Parallel loans enjoyed considerable popularity in the 1970s in the UK when they were frequently used to circumvent strict exchange controls. Also *back-to-back loan*.

partial lookback option   an option with a time 'window' of 30 or 60 days when the strike price is set or adjusted at the optimum level. After that, the option operates as normal. The cost of a partial lookback option falls between that of a conventional option and a lookback option because its window is for a limited period. See **lookback option**.

participation   similar to an option in structure, a participation contract includes a floor return and a reduced exposure to a favourable outcome on the underlying instrument, or a ceiling return with reduced exposure to an unfavourable outcome.

pass-through securities   securitised mortgages or other contracts where interest and principal are paid to the investors by an intermediary which has received these payments from the borrower. See **securitisation**.

payment netting   see **netting**.

payoff   the value of an option when it expires.

payoff diagram   a diagram showing an option's value at expiry relative to a range of underlying prices.

perpetual floating-rate note   a floating-rate note with no set maturity date.

plain vanilla   a description of a basic financial instrument, uncomplicated by *bells and whistles*. See **vanilla product**.

portfolio immunisation   managing a portfolio in a way that ensures the debt instruments in the portfolio cover a future liability.

position trading   holding strategic trading positions for a period rather than trading to cancel out positions at the end of each day.

positive carry   where the cost of an investment is less than the yield on the assets held; eg, securities are yielding 10 per cent and cost of funds is 8 per cent. See **negative carry**.

premium   in the context of options, the premium is the cost of buying an option; it represents the maximum amount the option-buyer can lose (and is likened to an insurance premium) and is income for the option seller (who also faces potentially unlimited risk and would hedge to cover that). A share or other security bought at a premium is bought for more than its par or face value. In foreign-exchange trading, a currency trading at a premium is worth more in the forward than in the spot market. Opposite is **discount**.

pre-settlement risk   the chance that something might go wrong in a transaction before it is settled; eg, a counterparty could go into liquidation.

program trading   a highly computerised method of trading and arbitraging between physical, futures and options markets, where buying or selling can be automatically triggered by specific market movements. It is used widely in the US, less in the UK, Japan and Australia. Program trading has been blamed in the US for disruptive falls in prices but rarely praised for raising or supporting price levels. See **triple witching hour**.

proprietary trading   trading as principal for a bank or investment bank's own account, as distinct from transactions on behalf of clients. In-house trading, or 'betting the bank'.

protected equity notes   see **All-Ordinaries Share Price Riskless Notes**.

put   see **option**.

put spread   a spread composed of a long position and a short position in puts on the same underlying instrument.

puttable swap   a swap contract which can be cancelled or terminated by either counterparty. See **callable swap**.

quantitative analyst   a mathematician who explains the characteristics of financial markets by using statistical models and formulas. *Abbrev.* **quant**.

quantity adjusting option   an option which generates a profit or loss in a currency different from that in which the option was dealt. *Abbrev.* **QUANTO**.

QUANTO   *abbrev.* **quantity adjusting option**.

QUANTO swap   a swap where the pay off is determined in one currency and paid in another, eg, a $US/DM swap 'quantoed' into sterling.

quant   quantitative analyst. See **rocket scientist**.

range forward contract   a type of forward contract used mostly in foreign-exchange trading, it combines the ability to take advantage of favourable movements in price with protection against unfavourable movements. Operates in a similar way to a collar on interest rates.

rate differential swap   a swap where one of the payment streams is denominated in a currency other than that of the notional principal amount. Also *cross-rate swap, diff swap.*

ratio option (spread)   an option spread where the number of contracts bought and sold are not equal, eg, selling one in-the-money call and buying two or three out-of-the money calls so that income received from the sale is used to buy more in-the-money calls.

redeemable warrant   a warrant offering cash redemption rather than a conventional exercise. Also *puttable warrant.*

reinvestment rate   the interest rate at which the cashflow from a coupon or principal payment can be reinvested.

repo   see **repurchase agreement**.

repurchase agreement   the sale of (usually government) securities to a purchaser who agrees to sell back the securities at an agreed future date and at an agreed price. Repos are popular because they are very low-risk. The Reserve Bank of Australia (in common with other central banks) uses repos in liquidity management, buying and selling securities to the market influence liquidity levels (see chapter 8). There is also substantial activity in repos among market-makers in fixed-interest securities. See **reverse repurchase agreement**.

reset swap   see **in-arrears swap**.

reverse dual-currency bond   a bond whose coupon is in a non-base currency and pays principal in the base currency. See **dual-currency bond, indexed currency option notes**.

reverse floater a type of structured security where the rate paid to the holder increases as floating rates decline (the return to the holder falls as the general level of interest rates rises). In 1986 the US's Sallie Mae (Student Loan Marketing Association) issued reverse floating-rate notes called 'Yield Curve Notes' which paid a coupon of 17.2 per cent less LIBOR. The coupon on the issue increased as LIBOR fell. Orange County made use of similarly structured notes (see chapter 9). See **bear floater**.

reverse repurchase agreement the opposite of repos; the Reserve Bank (central bank) sells securities to the market to drain off funds, or a client sells a repo to a bond dealer.

rho the sensitivity of an option's theoretical value to a change in interest rates. Represented by the Greek letter ρ.

risk arbitrage spread/yield curve plays which are closer to a low-level speculation than arbitrage.

rocket scientist one of Wall Street's *wunderkinder*, the geniuses of investment banking who invent the new financial and risk-management products, devise the money-spinning techniques based on options, futures and swaps. See **bells and whistles, quantitative analyst**.

rollercoaster swap an interest-rate swap whose notional principal fluctuates, generally to suit the financing requirements of a counterparty.

rolling hedge a continuous position in exchange-traded futures and options contracts, maintained by closing contracts as they near maturity and opening more distant ones.

SAFE *abbrev.* **synthetic agreement for foreign exchange**.

safe harbour a framework established by a regulatory body, such as the Australian Securities Commission, setting out circumstances under which certain trading activities may be carried out with minimal regulatory supervision.

SCOUT *abbrev.* **shared currency option under tender**.

securities lending a borrowing-lending process that does not require any movement of cash; the lender of the stock is paid a fee by the borrower who provides the lender with 'sub-stock' (substitution stock). Securities lending is popular with institutions which prefer to lend their stock rather than sell it under a repo arrangement, which is a buy-sell with cash changing hands.

securitisation converting an asset such as a loan into a marketable commodity by turning it into securities. The most popular form of securitisation involves mortgages which are pooled and sold, often in unitised form, enabling the lender to reliquefy the asset. Any asset that generates an income stream can be securitised—eg, mortgages, car loans, credit-card receivables.

series of options a group of options with the same exercise date, same strike price and of the same type, ie, put or call.

set-off when default arises, the right of the non-defaulting party to reduce its debt to the defaulter by the amount owed to it.

settlement date the future date of execution of a transaction; the time at which money and securities are to be exchanged.

settlement price the official closing price, established by the exchange at the close of each trading day and used by the clearing house as the basis for marking to market futures or over-the-counter contracts; or the price at which a transaction is settled. Also *delivery price*.

settlement risk the risk that a counterparty might not pay on time or as expected. Settlement risk is an incentive for netting. Also *delivery risk*. See **cross-currency settlement risk, netting**.

SFECH *abbrev.* **Sydney Futures Exchange Clearing House**.

shared currency option under tender insurance against the foreign-exchange risk associated with tendering for contracts involving different currencies. The party awarding the contract buys a currency option, and the cost of the premium is allocated among the tenderers in the same currency. When the tender is awarded the successful bidder receives the benefits of the option; each tendering party has paid a part of the cost. *Abbrev.* **SCOUT**.

share-price index futures   futures contracts based on an accepted stock exchange index, also known as *stock index futures*.

short hedge   a position taken to protect against a fall in prices.

short position   an excess of sales over purchases—in futures, to hold more sold than bought contracts. See **long position**.

single-currency swap   see **interest-rate swap**.

SOC   *abbrev.* **stop-on-close order**.

sovereign risk   see **country risk**.

speculator   a trader who uses a market purely to make a profit, who may not have any direct interest in or connection with the commodity traded. The speculator often takes a risk deliberately in the hope of reaping a handsome gain.

spot   in futures trading, the spot month is the nearest contract month traded and is usually the most active. In other markets, such as foreign exchange and gold, spot trading is today's trade, deliverable two days hence.

spread   the difference between the buying and selling rates (also the margin above a benchmark rate such as LIBOR). Investors hoping to profit from the narrowing or widening of the spread between different options use one or more of the various option spread strategies. See **intermonth spread, option spread, straddle**.

spread option   an option strategy to lock in an interest-rate spread. See **option spread**.

spread order   an order to buy or sell a series of options or futures, in a specified spread. The order is carried out only if the floor trader can secure the spread that has been requested.

spreadtion   see **spread option**.

STAGS   *abbrev.* **sterling transferable accruing government securities**.

standard deviation   in statistics, a measure of the spread of data; the degree to which observations differ from the mean.

step-down swap   an interest-rate swap with a drop in the fixed-rate payment over the life of the swap; or a type of amortising swap with successive reductions in the notional principal amount.

step-up cap   a cap that includes an incremental strike price at each rollover.

step-up swap   an interest-rate swap with an increase in the fixed rate at some point in the swap's life, or an accreting swap with successive increases in the notional principal amount.

step-up recovery FRNs   floating-rate bonds with interest calculated using a formula based on a theoretical ten-year US treasury bond. *Abbrev.* **SURFs**.

sterling transferable accruing government securities   the UK's version of the US's CATS (certificate of accrual on treasury securities) and TIGRs (treasury investment growth receipts); stripped UK gilts (government bonds). *Abbrev.*: **STAGS**. See **CATS, TIGRs**.

stochastic process   developing in accordance with a model built on probability; a mathematical process tracking the occurrence of a random phenomenon, often used to describe changes in the price of a security. Calculating stochastic processes is often the basis of a model for valuing options.

stock index futures   see **share-price index futures**.

stop-loss order   an instruction to a broker to sell if the market falls to a particular level or to buy if the market rises to a particular level. A sharp fall in prices can trigger stop-loss orders to sell and exaggerate an embryonic trend. Stop-loss orders are used more in futures and options trading than in the share market. Also *stop order*.

stop-on-close order   a futures market order left resting in the market so that if the stop-loss is activated within the last five minutes of trading the order is executed at market. *Abbrev.* **SOC**.

stop order   see **stop-loss order**.

straddle   a type of speculation in futures trading which calls for the simultaneous purchase in one delivery month and selling in another to take advantage of an expected change in the price differential between the two, or the simultaneous purchase or sale of a call option and put option with the same strike price and expiry date. A *negative straddle* is the opposite: the trader sells in the near month and buys in the distant month. (These strategies can be used to gain a tax advantage.) See **spread**.

strangle   the simultaneous purchase and sale of a call option and put option with the same expiry date but different strike prices.

strike price   the price at which an option may be exercised. The strike price, chosen by the buyer of the option, is set when the option contract is initiated. Also *exercise price*. See **option**.

strip hedge   a series of risk-management positions using forward or option contracts whose expiry dates suit the risk being hedged.

structured security   see **bear floater, inverse floater, reverse floater**.

SURFs   *abbrev.* **step-up recovery FRNs**.

swaps   the exchange of one entitlement for another. They can be interest-rate swaps (the larger category) or cross-currency swaps. With interest rate swaps two parties swap their form of borrowings (they do not exchange principal amounts) because the interest-rate structure of each suits the other better; for example, a borrower with fixed-rate funds would swap with another for floating-rate payments. Interest-rate swaps are used either to achieve lower borrowing costs or to gain entry to fixed-rate markets that would otherwise be inaccessible or too expensive. Interest-rate swaps can also be used to back up a view of interest rates, eg: a borrower may swap from fixed to floating rates if he or she believes that rates are likely to fall. See **amortising swap, annuity swap, asset-based swap, basis swap, blended interest-rate swap, callable swap, cocktail swap, commodity swap, cross-currency and interest-rate swap,**

deferred payment swap, delayed start swap, discount swap, dual-coupon swap, dual-currency swap, fixed-fixed currency swap, fixed-floating-rate swap, floating-floating swap, in-arrears swap, non-par swap, puttable swap, rate differential swap, reset swap, rollercoaster swap, step-down swap, step-up swap, unmatched swap, zero-coupon swap.

swap-driven   an issue described as swap-driven is a bond or note launched simultaneously with an agreement to a swap transaction.

swap rate   the fixed-rate payment on a swap.

swaption   see **interest-rate swap option**.

Sycom   *abbrev.* **Sydney Computerised Overnight Market**.

Sydney Computerised Overnight Market   an after-hours screen-trading system introduced by the Sydney Futures Exchange in November 1989 to enable contracts to be traded outside trading-floor hours. Much activity originates in New York and London. *Abbrev.* **Sycom**.

Sydney Futures Exchange   established in 1960 as the Sydney Greasy Wool Futures Exchange. The exchange was renamed in 1972 to reflect its diversification from wool. A cattle futures contract was introduced in 1975, followed by gold in 1978. The SFE became the first futures exchange outside the US to offer financial futures when, in 1979, it launched a 90-day bank bill futures contract. This was followed by the introduction of currency futures in 1980 and a share-price index futures contract in 1983. A ten-year government bond futures contract was launched in 1984, exchange-traded options began trading in 1985 and three-year bond futures arrived in 1988. Options are available on bank bills, government bonds and share-price-index futures. In 1994 the SFE launched Individual Shares Futures. In that year the exchange also announced a link with the New York Mercantile Exchange (Nymex) through which SFE members can trade Nymex's energy products including the West Texas Intermediate crude oil contract. See **Sydney Futures Exchange Clearing House, Sydney Computerised Overnight Market**.

Sydney Futures Exchange Clearing House   the clearing-house system developed by the SFE which began operating in December 1991. SFECH replaced the arrangement between the SFE and ICCH. *Abbrev.* **SFECH**.

synthetic agreement for foreign exchange   a forward-rate agreement in foreign currency which operates like a hedge contract for a specific period. *Abbrev.* **SAFE**.

synthetic option   a product that is created using forwards or futures to allow a company to control its losses on, say, interest rates or currencies, while still retaining the potential to make gains. A synthetic option uses a mix of forwards or futures and options to create a different option profile, for example buying futures and buying puts which gives the same result as buying a call outright but hopefully locks in a margin.

systemic risk   the risk of an event affecting the whole financial system. It arises from the threat of a chain reaction or domino effect if, say, a major institution fails, triggering the widespread calling-in of interlinked liabilities.

ten tola bar   a gold bar weighing 3.75 ounces, widely used in the Asian markets.

Texas hedge   a faulty strategy that increases the risk: what looked like a hedge (protection) turns out instead to increase the exposure.

tick movement   the minimum price movement in a futures contract, as defined by each contract's regulations. For example, a bank-bill price movement from 83.02 to 83.03 would be a 'one-tick movement'.

time decay   the loss of an option's value as it approaches its expiry date.

time value   in the context of options trading, this describes the difference between an option premium and the intrinsic value of an option; ie, the amount by which the option is in the money. Time value is affected by implied market volatility as well as the time remaining before the option expires. Also *extrinsic value*.

theta the rate at which the price of an option changes as time passes (time decay). Represented by the Greek symbol θ.

treasury investment growth receipts a type of zero-coupon US treasury bond which involves separating the interest and principal payments and selling each individually. *Abbrev.* **TIGRs**.

triple witching hour US market jargon for the close of trading on the Friday at the end of every quarter when stock options, futures options and futures contracts simultaneously expire. Volumes and volatility rise as traders and speculators close out their positions. Triple witching hour nervousness peaked in the mid-1980s; since then a combination of market changes and greater information flows has reduced its impact. See **program trading**.

tunnel see **collar**.

ultra vires outside legal authority or beyond the scope of an organisation. In the legendary Hammersmith & Fulham swaps case (see chapter 9) the UK's House of Lords deemed swaps activity *ultra vires* (outside the powers) of the local councils involved. See **Hammersmith & Fulham**.

uncovered writer see **naked option**.

underlying the asset, instrument, index or reference rate whose price movement determines the value of a derivative.

unmatched swap a swap agreement not matched by an asset or liability of either party, for example a swap undertaken as part of a swap dealer's warehousing activities.

unwinding reversing or closing out a position in, say, a swap.

value at risk the expected loss from an adverse market movement over a specified period, estimated using a probability analysis. Also *earnings at risk*.

vanilla product a straightforward financial instrument, such as a standard fixed-interest product with no sophisticated add-ons. Also *straight product*.

variable volume option an option written over more than one asset. If an aluminium producer wants to cover currency risk and the price of aluminium he or she may buy a currency option (call option if an exporter, put if an importer) linked to the aluminium price. The face value of the currency hedge is determined by the price of the second variable (the aluminium price) so if the aluminium price moves the currency cover has to be adjusted; if the currency moves, the aluminium delta is unchanged because the hedge is still covering the same face value amount of aluminium. This strategy involves correlation risk. See **correlation risk, delta, delta hedging**.

variation margin   see **margin call**.

vega   the rate at which the price of an option changes in relation to a small change in the volatility of the underlying asset or instrument.

vertical spread   see **option spread**.

volatility   erratic, mercurial change. In the context of the bond market, volatility describes the change in the price of a bond in relation to a given change in its yield to maturity. *Implied volatility* is the only component of the Black–Scholes option-pricing model which is not known at the outset. When an option has been traded the formula can be re-arranged to find the implied volatility at which the pricing model will calculate the traded price to be 'fair value'. *Historic volatility* is the annualised standard deviation of the relative rates of return of the daily closing prices for a security over a particular period.

warehousing   swaps market-makers' jargon for running a book of unmatched swaps rather than trying to pair each deal.

warrant   an option issued in the form of a security, usually written for a longer term. A warrant has the same function as an option: it provides the right to buy a specific amount of the underlying securities or shares, but is itself tradeable. Warrants are available in a range of types: a *debt warrant* is exercisable into a debt security, such as a bond or a note; an *equity warrant* is a warrant exercisable into an equity (share); a *killer warrant*, when exercised, automatically calls for the redemption of the security for which it was originally issued; a *naked warrant* is a debt warrant issued alone without a host (underlying) bond or security; and a *wedding warrant* is a structure of debt warrant attached to a host bond that protects the issuer from the potential doubling up of debt should the warrant be exercised. The warrants can only be exercised during the early part of their life into virgin bonds by tendering them along with the original callable bond. Also *harmless warrant*.

whipsaw   a sudden movement in price rapidly followed by an equally sudden reversal.

writer (of options)   the seller of the options, the party who grants the purchaser of the options the right to buy or sell the underlying asset or commodity at the agreed price.

yield curve   a graph showing the relationship betwen the yield to maturity and the term to maturity of a group of similar securities. A yield curve can be:
- **normal/positive/upward-sloping**, which reflects higher interest rates for longer-term investments;
- **downward/negative/inverse/inverted**, reflecting short rates higher than longer-term rates;
- **flat/horizontal**, suggesting little change in interest rates;
- **hump-backed**, indicating liquid conditions immediately followed by temporary tightness then a gradual decline in longer-term interest rates. Also *term structure of interest rates.*

zaitek   Japanese term for the financial markets activity of the treasurers of Japanese companies; the arbitrage and innovation behind new techniques such as futures, options and swaps which are used in various combinations to provide the cheapest possible funding and the highest possible return on investments. In the 1980s some companies made more money from zaitek than from their core business. Also *financial engineering, zaitech, zaiteku.*

zero-cost collar   a type of collar where a borrower arranges with his or her bank to buy a cap and sell a floor (vice versa in the case of an investor) so that the cost of the cap is completely offset by the income received from the floor. The borrower selects either the cap or the floor strike price and the bank calculates the other strike at which a zero cost is achieved. See **collar**.

zero-coupon bond   discounted bonds sold without a coupon. These bonds make no payment until maturity, when they are redeemed for face value.

zero-coupon swap   an interest-rate swap with the fixed-rate payment based on a zero-coupon bond. If the counterparty agrees, payment by the holder of the zero can be made in a single fixed sum at maturity while payments on the other leg can follow a conventional swap periodic-payments schedule. The payment mismatch raises the credit risk for one counterparty.

Part I

....

Instruments and Techniques

Figure 1.1: How derivatives derive in interest-rate and equity markets

INTEREST RATE MARKET	EQUITY MARKET
Primary market	Primary market

Governments and corporations issue securities to finance borrowings. They may be:

Issue of new shares by corporates for capital raising purposes

Short-term securities | Long-term securities | Equity securities

eg, Bank-bill NCDs

Commonwealth government bonds
Semi-government bonds
Corporate bonds

eg, Ordinary shares
Preference shares
Convertible notes

| Secondary market | Secondary market |

Short-term and long-term securities are actively traded between financial intermediaries (ie, banks and investors, fund managers and traders).

Shares are actively traded on the stock exchange by financial intermediaries, investors and traders.

| Derivatives market | Derivatives market |

Derivative products are introduced based on the underlying securities above.

Derivative products are introduced based on the underlying shares and sharemarket index.

Short-term interest rate derivatives | Long-term interest rate derivatives | Equity derivatives

eg, FRAs
Bank bill futures
Swaps

10-Year bond futures and options
3-Year bond futures & options
Swaps

eg, Share futures
All-Ordinaries share price index futures and options
Share options

Source: Sydney Futures Exchange

CHAPTER 1
· ·
THE DERIVATIVES EXPLOSION

A derivatives transaction is a contract whose value depends on (or derives from) the value of an underlying asset, reference rate or index.
Group of Thirty, Global Derivatives Study

Mention derivatives and most people wince, either because they associate these apparently esoteric instruments with stories of hair-raising losses or because they find the concept of derivatives baffling, or both. The collapse of the UK's 233-year-old blue-blood merchant bank, Barings PLC, in February 1995, following a more than $US1 billion futures-trading loss in its Singapore office brought derivatives an unprecedented and unwelcome level of worldwide publicity. Inadequate management control, rather than derivatives, seems to have been at the core of the issue (see chapters 9 and 10).

Derivatives would be less scary to many people if they were referred to by the more familiar labels of futures, forwards, options and swaps. The so-called exotic derivatives—swaptions, spreadtions, lookback options, knock-in options and so on—are variations on those concepts. Futures, forwards and options have been used for centuries. Swaps, which came to the fore in the 1980s, date from the 1960s and 1970s when they took the earlier, clumsier form of parallel loans. More recently, computer technology has enabled these age-old instruments to be traded at greater speed and, more relevantly, to be restructured in seemingly infinite variations.

Derivatives, because of their rapid growth and widespread use, have the capacity to make regulators nervous. They have also raised concerns in the legal and accounting professions. They have provided considerable work for lawyers as the legislators strive to keep the law in step with developments in the markets. Accountants have been kept busy devising new standards to cope with the taxation and accounting implications for companies using new-fangled hedging techniques and for banks selling and trading these products. Adequate disclosure of bank and corporate activity in derivatives is high on the accountants' wish-list.

Growth figures give a picture of derivatives' popularity. The US Government Accounting Office (GAO) suggests that the total notional value of outstanding derivatives contracts at the end of 1992 was at least $US17.6 trillion. However, measures of the face values give an exaggerated impression because derivatives do not involve a credit exposure to the full principal amounts but a settlement of net differences (some derivatives, such as foreign-currency swaps, do involve an exchange of comparable principal amounts but the continuing credit exposure is only to changes in the relative values of the two sides of the swap).

And even the multi-trillion-dollar face value in derivatives has to be seen in context: according to an article in the New York Federal Reserve's *Quarterly Review* (winter 1992–93) futures and option contracts traded on world exchanges totalled $US140 trillion in 1992. The Bank for International Settlements' *Central Bank Survey of Foreign Exchange Market Activity in April 1992* sets a figure of $US220 trillion on global net foreign-exchange turnover for 1992. Risk-exposure would be around only 2–4 per cent of the trillions in notional values in derivatives. The GAO commented: 'Because of the numerous combinations of products and types of risks, no single measure exists that reflects the actual amount at risk from derivatives activities.'

The rapid growth of derivatives would not be possible without technology, deregulation of the world's financial markets and the integration of those markets that technology has facilitated. Whereas in the cash or physical market tangible items are traded, be they wheat or gold or parcels of bank bills or shares, derivatives are financial transactions constructed out of these tangibles. Derivatives are not so much investments as tools which create exposures. These exposures may have been created for their own sake, to support a certain market view on, say, interest rates, or they may be to hedge an underlying exposure created in the normal course of business. Managing these exposures is a key element; no-one should be in derivatives with a casual approach. Using derivatives is not plain sailing—positions have to be constantly monitored and managed. And no-one denies there is a dark side to derivatives. To a large extent this has been created by the fact that derivatives have provided a convenient means for investors to leverage up on their expectations of, say, the direction of interest rates. Through leverage, an investor can gear up or leverage up: eg, by outlaying $10 receive returns commensurate with an outlay of, say, $50. Leverage is not reckless behaviour; wisely used, it enables low-cost risk management. But it can be risky business—fine when it works but potentially disastrous should the market take an unexpected and unwelcome turn.

Demand for risk-management products such as derivatives has increased because of volatility and uncertainty in interest rates, currencies and commodity and share prices. Derivatives have also become extremely popular because they are flexible and they involve less credit risk than lending or borrowing principal amounts. However, the proportional market risk for each dollar of initial margin on a futures contract is much higher than is the case with an investment in a physical security (because the gearing or leverage associated with futures allows a higher return or higher loss for every dollar invested). Derivatives are attractive because they incur extremely low transaction costs in relation to the face value of the contracts and, because the credit risk of derivatives is lower, the capital charge for banks is lower (ie, banks need less capital to support a derivative product than, say, a loan, see the Reserve Bank's *Prudential Supervision of Banks*, Attachment VI).

Trading and structuring derivatives requires the skills of a mathematician as well as those of a dealer. Treasury or capital markets areas of the banks and investment banks which market derivatives are staffed by traders who have to be quick to seize opportunities but also by mathematically inclined 'rocket-scientists' who are highly numerate, adept at maximising the capacities of a computer and capable of thinking laterally to devise ever-changing structures to suit clients' demands. It is this combination of the high-powered world of wholesale international finance, the skills of the computer age, the seemingly intangible nature of derivatives and vast sums of money involved that give derivatives such a threatening image. The fact that several companies and banks have lost money through derivatives has not helped assuage fears that derivatives hold the key to a potentially world-scale debacle.

The fault lies not with derivatives but with the users. Like any instrument falling into the wrong hands, derivatives can be dangerous. To quote the chairman of the US's Securities and Exchange Commission, Arthur Levitt, derivatives are not inherently bad or good. 'They are a bit like electricity,' he said. 'Dangerous if mishandled but bearing the potential to do tremendous good.' As some of the cases discussed in chapter 9 show, the combination of a complicated derivatives structure and leverage can be corporate dynamite.

The regulators and supervisors of financial markets around the world are anxious to ensure that the most pessimistic forecasts about derivatives do not come true—that a chain-reaction from a major player either defaulting or being the victim of a client's default does not escalate into a global financial disaster. To prevent this, the regulators and supervisors—and practitioners—have been working hard to keep pace with developments and practices in this still evolving market. Some market participants regard the regulators' concerns as overblown, others agree they are valid. No-one could argue, though, with the premise that the development of derivatives has put pressure on existing legislation, taxation and accounting regimes. A landmark report by the private-sector Group of Thirty's Global Derivatives Study Group, *Derivatives: Practices and Principles*, published in 1993, laid down a set of guidelines to be followed by the markets and these have been accepted as basic industry practice. However, the regulators and supervisors cannot legislate against greed and stupidity and these ingredients are generally present in large quantity in any financial disaster.

The nervousness generated by derivatives is regularly aired. In 1993 *Business Review Weekly* claimed that 'derivatives are what keep bank regulators awake at night'. The March 1994 issue of

Fortune likened derivatives to 'alligators in the swamp [lurking] in the global economy'. *The Economist* followed in May 1994 with the assertion that derivatives are 'the wild card in international finance'. An American academic, Professor Hu of the School of Law of the University of Texas, described derivatives as 'a Jurassic Park where new risks and uncertainties arise as financial creatures are invented, introduced and then evolve or mutate'. Colourful as these analogies are, they are not particularly helpful in defining derivatives or explaining their role in business and finance. Bad news always grabs more headlines than good. The many governments, government bodies and companies that have made prudent use of derivatives go about their business with their successes largely unsung; in the meantime, they are saving money for taxpayers and creating additional wealth for share-holders.

Derivatives are mainly used to manage market risk, ie, the risk arising from possible fluctuations in price. Using deriva-tives, traders can change exposure to a range of price risks relating to interest rates, currencies, equities or commodities without altering the underlying principal element of a transac-tion, in ways that may bring either reduced risk, a reduction in borrowing costs or an improvement in returns.

Derivatives can be used in portfolio management and in risk management—hedging, speculation and arbitrage. In practice, the distinction between these activities is not always clear-cut. Hedging is defined as taking a form of insurance to offset investment risk, speculation implies a high-risk strategy taken knowingly in anticipation of a gain (and recognising the possi-bility of a loss), and arbitrage involves riskless trading so as to profit from differences in the prices of a commodity or security in different markets.

OVER-THE-COUNTER AND EXCHANGE-TRADED

Derivatives fall broadly into two groups, in terms of the struc-ture of trading, settlement systems and characteristics of the contracts: over-the-counter (OTC) and exchange-traded deriva-tives. The distinction is important because each market carries

64   DERIVATIVES DECODED

different legal and credit-risk implications. OTC contracts are privately negotiated by banks and investment banks and their clients, and specifically tailored to customer needs, whereas exchange-traded derivatives are traded on a recognised exchange such as the Sydney Futures Exchange or the Australian Stock Exchange's derivatives market (ASXD), typically using a standard contract specification. Counterparty risk is much less of a concern for exchange-traded instruments because of the role of the clearing house (each trader's exposure is to the clearing house, not to another market participant) whereas with OTC derivatives counterparty risk is an important feature.

REPORTS ON DERIVATIVES

The now-famous comment made in January 1992 by the then president of the New York Federal Reserve, Gerald Corrigan, that 'you had all better take a very, very hard look at off-balance-sheet activities . . . I hope this sounds like a warning, because it is' prompted a rush to scrutinise derivatives—this burgeoning corner of the global financial markets. A common objective of subsequent reports was to strip away the hysteria that had accompanied much commentary on derivatives and seriously examine the risks they presented. Thus the reports did not focus on the trillions of dollars outstanding on derivatives but instead discussed the associated risks, how to identify and measure them and ensure that risk-management systems were in place to reduce the possibility of fraud, a costly blunder or, worse, systemic risk.

Report by the Group of Thirty

In 1992, in the wake of Corrigan's warning, the Group of Thirty (G30) formed a study group to try to shed some light on derivatives, widely regarded as complex and esoteric instruments. The result was the report released in 1993 by the Group of Thirty's Global Derivatives Study Group. As Paul Volcker, chairman of the Group of Thirty, notes in his foreword to *Derivatives: Practices and Principles*, there was considerable demand for an unofficial but authoritative review of industry practices and performance. Volcker wrote: 'In the light of the Group of Thirty's past success in sponsoring work on important but technically abstruse financial questions, the Group appeared a natural place for launching such an effort.'

The G30 study has made a significant contribution towards allaying fears and encouraging discipline and caution in the use of derivatives. A key element of the report is its definitive set of 24 recommended risk-management practices for dealers and end-users. These have come to be regarded as the industry blueprint; however, as the report modestly notes, they are not the only means to good management. 'What they do offer is a benchmark against which participants can measure their own practices', the report says. The first two recommendations relate to the role of senior management and the need for dealers to mark their derivatives positions to market at least daily for risk-management purposes. To assist in this, the Australian Financial Markets Association publishes end-of-day valuation rates, initially for users of swaps and options. The rate is shown on Telerate pages 45400 and onwards. Among other factors, the G30 also stressed the benefits of netting, in terms of helping reduce settlement risks and credit exposures.

Regulators' concerns about derivatives have been prompted by the market's rapid growth, the risks involved and whether or not these represent new challenges. The associated risks—market, credit, systemic, operational, legal, accounting, tax and regulatory—are the subject of widespread discussion. The G30 concluded that the risks associated with derivatives are not new, noting: 'They are the same kinds of risks found in traditional products.'

Report by the US Government Accounting Office

In 1994 the US Government Accounting Office issued a report which called for greater regulation. The GAO, which focused on four basic types of derivatives—forwards, futures, options and swaps—chiefly sought to determine:

- what risks derivatives might pose to individual firms and to the financial system and how firms and regulators were attempting to control these risks;

- whether gaps and inconsistencies existed in US regulation of derivatives;
- whether existing accounting rules resulted in financial reports that provided market participants and investors with adequate information about firms' use of derivatives; and
- what the implications of the international use of derivatives were for US regulation.

GAO's recommendations to Congress included federal regulation of the safety and soundness of all major US OTC derivatives dealers. GAO said:

> The immediate need is for Congress to bring the currently unregulated OTC derivatives activities of securities firm and insurance company affiliates under the purview of one or more of the existing federal financial regulators and to ensure that derivatives regulation is consistent and comprehensive across regulatory agencies . . . Congress [should] systematically address the need to revamp and modernise the entire US financial regulatory system. Gaps and weaknesses in OTC derivatives regulation clearly demonstrate that the existing regulatory structure has not kept pace with the dramatic and rapid changes in the domestic and global financial markets that have occurred over the past several years.

GAO also made several recommendations to regulators, to the Federal Accounting Standards Board (FASB) and to the Securities and Exchange Commission (SEC), stressing *inter alia* the need for accurate and centralised information, adequate capital standards, adequate disclosure and fair valuation of derivatives, good internal controls, and comprehensive, consistent accounting rules and disclosure requirements.

Reserve Bank survey

In March 1994, the Reserve Bank of Australia initiated a survey of banks' activities in derivatives. The Reserve Bank sought information about products traded by banks, the maturity mix of banks' portfolios and counterparties, banks' strategies in derivatives markets and their risk-management practices. The RBA survey yielded the following figures:

Table 1.1   Banks' derivatives activity (contracts outstanding March 1994)

	Notional principal $m	Credit equivalent $m
Foreign exchange		
Forwards	724 649	27 513
Futures	932	0
Options	80 614	1 414
Cross-currency interest-rate swaps	77 849	7 920
Total	884 044	36 847
Interest rates		
Forward-rate agreements	309 546	489
Futures	315 148	0
Swaps	532 379	13 969
Options	177 913	611
Total	1 334 986	15 069
Other markets		
Precious metals	12 043	490
Energy products	316	14
Base metals	4 474	88
Stocks and sharemarket indices	35 440	10
Total	52 274	602
TOTAL	2 271 304	52 518

Source: Reserve Bank study: *Australian banks' Activities in Derivatives Markets: Products and Risk-Management Practices*

The notional principal figures need to be viewed with caution. When two reporting banks engage each other as counterparties in a derivatives transaction, the value of this transaction is counted twice.

Australian Securities Commission report

The Australian Securities Commission (ASC) released its report on over-the-counter (OTC) derivatives in May 1994. The ASC's report, like that of the G30, focused on OTC derivatives. This reflects the existing thorough regulation of exchange-based derivatives and the prevailing grey areas in the regulation of the OTC markets. The ASC's report proposed that a three-tier regulatory framework be applied to OTC derivatives transactions—differentiating between wholesale transactions privately negotiated, wholesale 'tradeable' transactions and retail transactions. As an interim step, the ASC implemented a 'safe-harbour' exemption from regulatory controls for transactions involving sophisticated professionals, provided they were subject to supervision regarding capital standards. The report also outlined major concerns such as legal uncertainty, protection of 'retail' customers and the need to ensure orderly markets to reduce systemic risk, and canvassed outstanding law-reform issues.

Australian Financial Markets Association survey

In June 1994 the Australian Financial Markets Association released the findings of a survey of risk management of derivatives in Australia. The purpose of the survey, focusing on portfolio valuation and the measurement of market risk and credit risk, was to compare Australian practice with the 'market best practice' guidelines set out in the G30's report. Australian dealers were rated as having world-class standards of professionalism. According to the survey results:

- Australian dealers place a great deal of importance on derivatives for risk-management purposes;
- most have already undertaken internal evaluations to compare their controls with the G30 recommendations; and
- Australian banks dealing in derivative markets tend to be ahead of their international counterparts in many respects. This holds particularly true for systems-related issues such as systems integration and the internal development of systems, tailored to suit the business needs of the individual organisations.

Corporate derivatives study: Australian Society of Corporate Treasurers and Price Waterhouse

In September 1994 Price Waterhouse, in association with the Australian Society of Corporate Treasurers, commissioned an Australian study of corporate (end-user) use of derivatives. The survey distinguished between treasuries which hedge an underlying exposure and leave the hedge in place until the underlying exposure matures, and active hedgers where the level of hedging varies to take advantage of opportunities for profit. 'This distinction was made because the two different types of treasuries have significantly different requirements', the report states. 'The active hedger needs more sophisticated systems, more timely information and stricter controls as the level of risk is much greater.' In general, the survey concluded that corporate users had a 'healthy respect' for derivatives. However, two areas of concern emerged:

- the level of senior management knowledge. More than 20 per cent of the respondents indicated that there was a sizeable gap between the level of knowledge of treasury staff and that of senior management, raising the question of how senior management could appropriately monitor and control the risks associated with derivatives; and
- systems capability. With some corporates the systems in place were not able to capture and record some of the newer transactions undertaken. If the transactions could not be entered into the systems, evaluating, managing and monitoring associated risks become very difficult.

AIMA/SFE survey of derivatives usage by Australian fund managers

The survey, conducted by the Australian Investment Managers' Association, sponsored by the Sydney Futures Exchange and released in November 1994, found that Australian fund managers take a 'conservative but active approach' to derivatives. 'Exchange-traded derivatives are preferred to over-the-counter derivatives since established regulation and valuation policies are already in place for the former', the survey noted. According to the survey, the most widely used equity derivative product was the SFE's share-price index futures contract (used by 91 per cent of respondents), followed by the ASX's equity option contracts (used by 81 per cent of respondents). The most widely used interest-rate derivative was the SFE's three-year and ten-year bond futures and options contracts, used by 88 per cent of respondents. 'Products such as FRAs and interest-rate swaps which are commonly used in the banking industry are not used significantly by the fund management industry', the survey said.

Exotic products were also found to be used by very few respondents.

The growth of the markets is graphically illustrated by the expansion of activity in the years from 1991 to 1994 (see figure 1.2).

Earlier reports were by the US's Commodity Futures Trading Commission (CFTC) (*Derivative Markets and their Regulation*, 1993), the Bank of England (*Derivatives Working Group Report*, 1993) and the Bank for International Settlements (BIS) (*Recent Developments in International Interbank Relations*, 1992). The central conclusion of the CFTC's report was that while there seemed to be no need for fundamental changes in the regulatory structure because of the growing use of OTC derivatives, greater coordination among federal financial regulators would add to confidence that federal oversight remained adequate. The CFTC also supported the establishment of an interagency council comprising the SEC, CFTC and bank regulators to supplement efforts for greater cooperation, information-sharing and harmonisation of regulations. The Bank of England's working group commented that many of the problems thrown up by derivatives are common to new markets, eg, lack of data, absence of standardised market practices, untested areas of the law, possibly shallow and volatile markets, a lag between product innovation and management of risk and an insufficient spread of necessary skills. The Bank of England's recommendations included as the two most substantive:

- that research on the relative price volatility and liquidity of cash and derivative markets should be conducted, with a view to improving understanding of the increasing links between financial markets, and their potential systemic implications; and
- that the Bank of England, in consultation with the BIS, considers which data on exchange-traded and OTC derivative markets it is desirable to collect for the purposes of examining market size and the degree of concentration, and subsequently considers establishing a survey of the derivative markets comparable to that already conducted for foreign-exchange activity.

Figure 1.2 The OTC derivatives markets

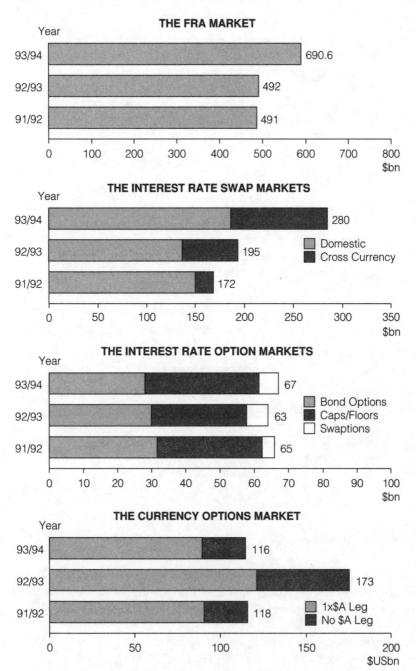

Source: AFMA's 1994 Australian Financial Markets Report, prepared by the Financial Products Research Group

Figure 1.3 Exchange-traded derivatives markets

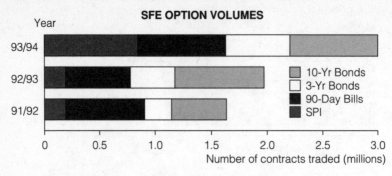

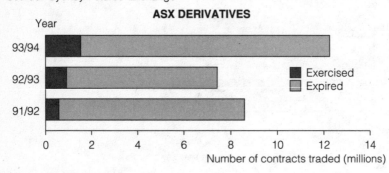

Source: Sydney Futures Exchange

Source: ASX Derivatives

The BIS report, which pointed out that since the mid-1980s, growth in turnover and volumes outstanding in derivatives had outpaced that of most other financial activity, discussed:

- credit concerns;
- the complexity of risks incurred in OTC derivatives which has intensified demand for advanced hardware and software systems and for highly-skilled staff;

- the growing concentration of funds in certain types of institutions which trade actively, which has increased the potential for some large players to affect market prices;
- the strengthened linkages between markets following more rapid dissemination of information;
- widespread use of derivatives; and
- the more complex strategies that can be structured.

The BIS supported enhancing netting schemes and favoured greater harmonisation of accounting and reporting practices for off-balance-sheet instruments. It also highlighted the dangers associated with legal uncertainties and cited the new challenges to the traditional role of central banks in fostering financial market stability. The report said:

> Central banks must [also] work with other financial authorities to help ensure that banks and other financial institutions are adequately capitalised and have appropriate systems in place for managing and controlling risks. Beyond this, it is clear that in order to play an effective supporting role in further reducing risks, central banks need to continue to develop further their understanding of the nature of financial activities and of the risks faced individually and collectively by all participants in financial markets.

HOW DERIVATIVES BENEFIT THE ECONOMY*

Properly applied, derivatives offer very real benefits and have a genuine role to play in risk management, as the following examples show.

Airline

An airline is in the unusual position of operating with a highly mixed receivables side in its balance sheet, with ticket income flowing in a variety of currencies, the mix constantly changing and the volume unpredictable. Its shareholders' funds would be denominated in its domestic currency, as would most expenses and wages. However, an airline also has to cope with significant fuel costs so it watches the oil price carefully. It also watches its competitors carefully, because the behaviour of competitors is an important element in any company's approach to hedging. Hedging at a time when your competitors are not and then finding the hedge unnecessary (because prices have moved in your favour) is a costly exercise. The management and board of an airline have no control over the unknowns, such as how many passengers they will carry in a year, but they can take steps, including using derivatives, to manage risks such as the company's exposure to currency fluctuations and to changes in the price of oil.

Bank

Banks borrow and lend, activities which can produce a structural mismatch in their balance sheets. They offer products such as fixed-rate home loans (a bank's assets) while they take deposits (its liabilities) at variable rates. In 1994, as the cost of home loans began to rise, customers increasingly wanted to borrow at fixed rates to lock in a known cost for at least a few years. On the other side, depositors could also see further increases in interest rates on the horizon and so became reluctant to place funds in fixed deposits, preferring to lodge their funds where the interest rate would change in line with the market. The reverse applies when interest rates are falling: borrowers want floating rates that shift in line with the market but depositors want to fix the rate rather than see their returns fall. Banks use interest-rate swaps, mostly fixed-to-floating, and the interest-rate futures market to hedge the exposures they incur as a result of the mismatch in rates.

Mining house

Mining houses live with volatility in the prices of the resources they dig out of the ground, often unpredictable costs of production and equally unknown but frequently high exploration costs. Moreover, their timetable of production can be uncertain. A gold-mining house could be anticipating a production flow in six months' time but that could be delayed and meanwhile the spot price of gold could drop from $500 to $300. Mining houses offset some of the uncertainty by selling a proportion of their production forward but they cannot commit 100 per cent of production in case forecasts prove wrong. Mining companies make prudent use of the forward market for their production, generally adhering to fairly straightforward hedging techniques.

Other sectors of the Australian economy also use derivatives to hedge. For example, the government sector might borrow in yen rather than $A and hedge its currency exposure so that, even allowing for hedging expenses, the borrowing has been made at a lower cost than could have been achieved in $A. That is a saving for the Australian taxpayer. Many state government infrastructure projects have been facilitated by the borrower's ability, through the swaps market, to raise foreign-currency funds and swap back into $A finance. State governments use derivatives essentially to generate cheaper funding, again a benefit to taxpayers. Also, by borrowing overseas and swapping back into $A, a state government borrower can not only achieve lower funding costs but also gain access to a wider market, and so can raise funds at a time when a similar scale of borrowing might be difficult in the smaller Australian market. The chief risk relates to the swap counterparty but states deal only with the top-rated banks.

Using an interest-rate swap, many borrowers have been able to solve the impasse between their desire for fixed-rate funds and a bank's inclination to lend only floating-rate finance.

Companies look at derivatives with a different perspective from, say, a bank. A company manufacturing widgets might use derivatives to improve its returns on equity and increase balance-sheet efficiency but its main business is still making widgets. Chiefly, companies are looking to protect against interest-rate, foreign-exchange and commodity risk.

Fund managers, as buyers of securities, are exposed to interest-rate, foreign-exchange and equity-price movements and use derivatives such as swaps to improve their returns.

* This section is adapted from an address by Ian Moore, executive vice-president, Bankers Trust Australia Limited, to an ASFA conference in November 1994.

CHAPTER 2
. . . .
FUTURES

Derivatives in the form of futures and forward contracts are far from new. Futures and forwards are used chiefly for risk management (hedging) but also for investment (trading). Risk management enables those operating in markets to protect the value of their assets—shares or bonds—against changes in price and capital value. Traders and speculators use derivatives to make a profit; unlike the hedgers, they have no position in the underlying assets but use derivatives because they offer lower transaction costs and the chance for leverage, ie, gaining a large exposure to an underlying asset for a small initial outlay. Hedgers use futures to reduce risk; traders accept the 'unwanted' risk of hedgers and use futures to try to make a profit. A trader with a view in the physical market would also have a view in futures, so the deeper the physical market the deeper the corresponding futures market is likely to be.

DEVELOPMENT AND GROWTH

Futures or forward markets have existed for centuries, initially based on rural commodities such as grains, beef or wool. Futures exchanges in the form we know today developed in the United States during the nineteenth century; the Chicago Board of Trade was established in 1848 and was followed by the Chicago Butter and Egg Board which, in 1919, changed its name to the Chicago Mercantile Exchange. The success of the Chicago exchanges led to the growth of other exchanges in the US and elsewhere, dealing in cotton, grains, coffee, sugar and cocoa. Until the 1970s, futures markets dealt mostly in commodities. The Sydney Futures Exchange (SFE), founded in 1960 as the Sydney Greasy Wool Futures Exchange, traded only wool until the cattle contract was introduced in 1975. A gold contract was launched in 1978 and in the following year the SFE was the first exchange outside the US to follow that country's lead in financial futures when it launched the 90-day bank-bill futures contract.

Financial futures were the product of the global economic upheavals of the 1970s. Successive increases in the price of oil, fluctuating interest rates, rising inflation and the switch from fixed to floating exchange rates focused attention on the need to protect against unforeseen movements in interest rates and currencies and, more recently, share prices.

Financial futures have been the source of growth in the futures industry over the past two decades. Initiated in 1972 in Chicago, in the form of currency futures, financial futures have increased in popularity, as evidenced by the proliferation around the world of new futures exchanges concentrating on financial instruments. Financial futures are based on a range of instruments representing interest rates, currencies and share-price indexes. The markets are increasingly international in nature, with exchanges in Asia linked to those in Europe and the US. In 1989 the SFE introduced Sycom (Sydney Computerised Overnight Market), a computerised screen-dealing system which provides access, through SFE members, to the exchange's futures and options contracts when the trading floor is closed, thus enabling Australian investors to trade the SFE's contracts when the major markets in the US and Europe are open. In 1994 the SFE announced a trading link with the giant New York Mercantile Exchange (Nymex), enabling the SFE to trade Nymex's energy contracts. A particular attraction is Nymex's extremely liquid West Texas Intermediate (WTI) crude oil contract.

USERS

The chief users of financial futures are:

- institutions which generate financial instruments (eg, bills of exchange, bonds and shares);
- those who trade the financial instruments (banks, investment banks, investment institutions and some individuals);
- borrowers and lenders, fund managers, importers, exporters and manufacturers; and
- investors and speculators.

Virtually any business can find a use for financial futures at some time. Banks, investment banks, life offices and other financial institutions, borrowers and lenders and so on use financial futures to hedge, or insure, against unfavourable movements in prices. Financial futures are also used by traders, either investing or speculating. Speculators are important—their intervention, as well as stimulating trading, provides a self-correcting mechanism for the market. And speculators and traders take on the risks the hedgers are trying to avoid.

Banks and investment banks have the capacity to create financial instruments, such as forward-rate agreements (FRAs, see chapter 3) and swaps, whose pricing is normally based on a corresponding financial futures contract and, in their daily business, they trade the instruments, shares and currencies that underlie futures contracts. Likewise, companies issue shares to raise capital, the shares are traded on the stock exchange and are the underlying instruments for share futures and options. Banks, investment banks and companies which deal or trade in financial instruments are the financial markets' equivalent of the farmers harvesting wheat and hedging on the Chicago exchanges, or gold producers hedging the precious metal on the New York Commodity Exchange (Comex). Companies and other organisations using financial instruments are therefore natural hedgers in the financial futures market although they often engage in active speculation to try to maximise their investment returns.

FUTURES CONTRACT

A futures contract is a binding obligation, enforceable at law, requiring delivery of a specific quantity of a specific type of good, at an agreed price, place and time. Every contract has a buyer and a seller. A futures contract can be terminated at any time before it is due for delivery by selling (if the trader were holding a bought contract) or buying (if the trader were holding a sold contract). Most futures contracts are closed out before delivery date; generally, only about 3 per cent of contracts run to physical delivery of the instrument on which the contract is based. All SFE contracts, except 90-day bank-bill futures, are terminated by cash-settlement and not physical delivery. This, however, could change, with the SFE investigating the possibility of making its two bond-futures contracts deliverable.

Bank-bill futures

The contract unit in the bank-accepted bill futures contract is $A500 000 worth of 90-day bank-accepted bills of exchange (the SFE has signalled its intention to double the size of the contract to $1 million). Suitable stock for delivery can be either five bank-accepted bills each of $A100 000 or one bill of $A500 000 or the equivalent amounts in bank certificates of deposit (CDs, which are treated by the market as having the same credit risk as bank bills of exchange). The bills or CDs must mature between 85 and 95 days from settlement date of the contract and, if bills, must have the same drawer, acceptor and due date, and be endorsed by the seller (deliverer).

Bank bills are quoted in prices in futures trading, not in terms of yield as they are in the physical market. This puts them on the same basis for quoting as other futures contracts. The bank-bill futures price is calculated by deducting the yield from 100: for example, a yield of 8 per cent would translate into a price of 92.00 (100 less 8). The seller looks for a higher price (lower yield) and the buyer looks for a lower price (higher yield). It is important to clarify whether a trader is referring to a yield or a price movement in bank-bill futures, because when one rises the other falls as table 2.1 shows:

Table 2.1   SFE 90-day bank-bill futures

Yield %	Price	Contract value $
5	95.00	493 910.69
10	90.00	487 967.91
20	80.00	476 501.31

The minimum amount the price can move is 0.01, eg, 90.00 to 90.01 or one basis point which is the same as 0.01 per cent in yield terms. As with other futures contracts, a minimum initial margin (deposit) is required on the bank-bill futures contract. Interest is paid by the clearing house on this deposit. The level of the initial margin is set by the Sydney Futures Exchange Clearing House (SFECH) and varies in line with market movements. If the price of the financial instrument moves against a trader—rises from the seller's price or falls from the buyer's— then margin calls (or variation margins) can be made by the clearing house on all clearing members. They in turn call their clients for the funds. This is done to cover any risk associated with the movements in price. The additional funds requested by way of margin calls are a safeguard to ensure that sufficient funds are available should a paper loss become a real loss. Once a paper loss is reversed the margin call is refunded. Unlike the initial margin, funds lodged through margin calls do not attract interest.

Government bond futures

Government or treasury bond futures contracts provide a method for bond-traders and investors to protect their investments against unfavourable movements in interest rates (bond yields). The SFE offers two government bond contracts: a three-year and a ten-year contract, both based on $A100 000 face value and carrying a notional 12 per cent coupon. The 10-year bond futures contract is particularly useful to institutions such as life offices and pension funds which hold long bonds.

Bond futures are quoted in a similar way to bank-bill futures, with the yield-per-cent-per-annum deducted from 100, so that a bond yielding 9.5 per cent per annum would be quoted at a price of 90.50. Bond futures are not a deliverable contract (although this is likely to change); settlement of contracts still held at the end of a trading period takes place in cash. The cash-settlement price is calculated using the average of buying and selling quotes provided against a basket of physical commonwealth bonds by twelve major bond-dealers, chosen at random on the last morning of trading. These random quotes are taken at three times during the morning session, at 9.45, 10.30 and 11.15am, and then averaged. The two highest and two lowest buying quotes, and two highest and two lowest selling quotes for each bond in the basket, are omitted from the calculation. An official settlement price, which takes into account the prices calculated, is published at 3pm that day.

Share-price index futures

Share-price index (SPI) futures are a substitute for holding a diversified portfolio of shares. So these futures contracts are useful for anyone, an individual or a corporate, looking for protection against losses that could arise from price changes in the sharemarket. The contract also provides a guide to expectations about share prices.

The SPI futures contract is based on the Australian Stock Exchange's (ASX) All-Ordinaries index—the barometer of the Australian sharemarket. The All-Ordinaries index is calculated using the market prices of more than 250 companies listed on the ASX. The market value of these companies adds up to about 90 per cent of the value of all listed shares. The index is calculated continuously through the trading day and is published daily at the close of trading. Traders should bear in mind that the All-Ordinaries is only a *price* index—it does not take account of dividends, so holding share-price index (SPI) futures is not an exact substitute for holding shares.

The unit of the share-price index futures contract equals the All-Ordinaries index multiplied by $25; if the index were 1900, the contract value would be $47 500 ($25 x 1 900). Ten SPI contracts would be equivalent to a share portfolio with a face value of $475 000. The share-price index futures contract is another non-deliverable contract, with settlement taking place in cash. The price for cash-settlement is the closing quote, taken to one decimal place, for the All-Ordinaries index on the last day of trading.

Individual Share Futures

Individual Share Futures (ISFs) traded on the Sydney Futures Exchange since May 1994, are futures contracts based on the shares of individual listed companies. ISFs are available on blue-chip companies such as BHP, National Australia Bank,

News Corporation, BTR Nylex, MIM Holdings, Westpac Banking Corporation and Western Mining. Each contract is based on 1000 shares of the underlying stock (although the contract size can be altered, to take account of capital reconstructions, eg, share splits, bonus issues, rights issues). So if BHP shares are trading at $20, one BHP share futures contract would be worth $20 000. For an initial margin (outlay) of around $400–$600 a buyer has exposure to 1000 shares in a blue-chip stock. Share futures contracts are cash-settled against the price of the underlying share—there is no physical delivery of shares when the contract expires. Profits or losses are credited or debited to the account of the holder of the contract by the Sydney Futures Exchange Clearing House (SFECH). However, as is generally the case in futures trading, most contracts are not held to expiry but cancelled by taking an equal and opposite position.

How financial futures are traded

Futures trading is open to anyone who has a view about the future direction of, say, interest rates or share prices. Users of futures markets fall into three overlapping categories: producers or users (who are essentially hedgers), speculators and arbitragers. The producers and users trade futures to hedge or protect against unfavourable price movements. The speculators may have no direct interest in, say, government bonds or shares, but trade in the expectation of making profits. The arbitragers aim to profit specifically from anomalies between the physical and futures market prices.

An example of a speculator is a local; locals are professional individual traders operating on the floor of the exchange on their own account, rather than as a broker acting on behalf of clients. Local members must be sponsored by an SFE floor member and are also required to have a member of SFECH clear the trades they execute. Individuals and companies not wishing to become local members can use an associate or floor-member firm to deal on their behalf. When an associate-member firm is used, contracts placed through the associate are passed to floor members and the brokerage shared. Floor-member firms have traders on the floor of the Sydney Futures Exchange executing orders by open outcry on behalf of clients in much the same way that sharebrokers had their traders on the floor of the stock exchange before sharetrading became automated through SEATS (Stock Exchange Automated Trading System). A client can instruct the futures broker to buy, sell, switch or carry out a range of other orders. Traders gather on the floor of the SFE in pits, with each actively traded contract having its own pit.

Sydney Computerised Overnight Market (Sycom)

Since 1989 Sycom has enabled SFE trading to take place during hours when the trading floor is closed. Sycom trades from 4.40pm until 7am (4pm New York time) and all major contracts listed by the SFE are traded on the system through floor members of the exchange. Sycom operates through personal computers linked to the SFE's mainframe computer. By the end of 1994 10 per cent of the SFE's turnover was traded on Sycom.

Hedging

Hedging involves taking an opposite and equal position in the physical and futures markets, with the objective of compensating in one market for potential losses in another. Total elimination of risk would require perfect correlation between the physical and futures markets—possible only in theory. The imperfect correlation between the two is known as *basis risk*, being the price relationship between the physical and futures markets.

A hedge can be either to buy (long) or to sell (short). In the case of a long hedge, a future buyer of, say, bonds, or lender of funds, sets a rate of return now on a forward investment. The long hedge can be used to protect against a possible fall in interest rates. An investor or lender is able to fix the return on funds by buying futures contracts for forward delivery. If rates drop between the purchase date and delivery date, the resulting futures profit will help offset the drop in interest rates over the period, thus cushioning a loss of revenue (offsetting an opportunity cost).

As the example below shows, by using 10–year bond futures to hedge the cost of the future acquisition of physical bonds the portfolio manager is able to obtain protection from the 0.50 per cent drop in bond yields (rise in bond prices or higher entry cost)—and in fact generates a small gain of $2169.18 (the difference between the futures profit and the additional amount that had to be paid for bonds in March, ie, $288 498.50 – $286 329.32). Had yields risen (prices fallen) between January and March, the portfolio manager would have lost on the futures trade but would have been able to buy physical bonds for a lower outlay.

In January, a portfolio manager knows that in March he or she will have $10 million to invest and that these funds will be used to buy bonds. The manager wants to lock in the bond price that would have been received had the $10 million been available for investment now.

Physical bond market	10-year bond futures
Buying $10 million face value of 10% October 2002 bonds at the prevailing yield of 10.25%. Current market value of bonds is $9 855 033.58	Buys 85* March 10-year bond futures at a price of 89.800 (10.2%) to hedge future purchase of physical bonds. Market value $9 445 326.65
March	
Manager buys $10 million face value 10% October 2002 bonds at a yield of 9.75%, costs $10 141 362.90, or $286 329.32 more than if the bonds had been bought in January	Bond yields have fallen. Manager sells 85* March 10-year bond futures at 90.300 (9.7%) to close futures position. Market value: $9 733 825.15. Profit on futures trade: $288 498.50

* number of contracts required to accurately match dollar value movements in the futures hedge with the phsyical bonds to be purchased.

In the case of a short hedge, a borrower would fix the cost of future borrowed funds by selling a bank-bill futures contract in anticipation of the instrument being, at the future date, at a higher yield (lower price) than the current futures contract price.

A borrower uses a selling hedge to offset the effects of rising interest rates. The borrower of funds can sell a futures contract, so that if interest rates move higher (the price falls) between the hedge date and delivery of the futures contract, then the value of the contract drops and the hedger makes a gain by buying back the contract at the lower price (higher yield). The profit on the futures transaction goes towards offsetting the rise in interest rates during the same period.

Banks and investment banks which run large bill portfolios and which both trade and create bills of exchange use bank-bill futures to hedge their risk. Likewise, finance companies and large corporations which also hold and trade bills are attracted to bank-bill futures while holders of government bonds, such as banks, life offices, superannuation funds and insurance companies use bond futures to hedge their holdings of commonwealth and semi-government bonds.

Arbitrage

Arbitragers enter a market to take advantage of discrepancies in prices resulting from temporary imbalances in supply or demand or time-lags in market response to an event or announcement. An arbitrager identifes an opportunity, comes in to buy or sell (buying if the price is low, selling if the price is high), thereby pushing up a low price or reducing a high price and so bringing prices back into equilibrium. To qualify as arbitrage, the process of simultaneous buying and selling has to involve two markets, eg cash and futures.

A cash-futures arbitrage would involve simultaneous transactions in two markets for securities which have similar pricing characteristics. When prices for futures contracts, allowing for the cost of carry, are greater than cash prices, an arbitrager buys the securities or commodities in the cash market and sells futures contracts (a long arbitrage). When prices for futures, allowing for the cost of carry, are less than those in the cash market, an arbitrager sells securities or commodities in the cash market and buys futures contracts (a short arbitrage). Arbitragers often do not hold a position for long; the position is closed as soon as the price relationship returns to normal, ending an arbitrager's interest.

Risks for an arbitrager are generally limited to a change in financing costs and the price risk associated with executing the various transactions involved.

Speculation

A speculator aims to buy low and sell high. A speculator is not involved in the physical instrument or commodity traded but trades merely in anticipation of making a profit through a fairly high-risk strategy, while acknowledging that there is potential to make a loss. For example, a speculator might buy share-price index futures contracts in expectation of a price rise so that the position could later be closed by selling the contracts at a higher price for a profit:

October 10

Cash market	Futures market
No transaction. All-Ordinaries index at 1 900.0	Speculator buys 10 December SPI futures at market price of 1 905.0, value $476 250.00

October 25

Cash market	Futures market
No transaction. All-Ordinaries index has risen to 1 950.0	Speculator sells 10 December SPI futures at new market price of 1 957.0, value $489 250.0

Speculator's profit is $13 000, ie, $489 250.00 – $476 250.00, or 52 points x 10 contracts x $25 a point.

Profits to a speculator holding contracts that are increasing in value accumulate in the speculator's account with his or her futures broker; these profits result from the margin calls made daily to the party holding the opposite position to the speculator.

Spread trading

Spread trading involves simultaneously buying and selling two different futures contracts, with the trader hoping to anticipate correctly the likely change in the relative values of the two contracts. Spread trading can be *intermonth* (buying and selling different contract months of the same commodity) or *intercommodity* (using different commodities).

With an intermonth spread the objective is to buy the month expected to increase in value and sell the month expected to fall. To be successful, the trader has to understand what influences the price differentials.

For example, a bank-bill trader has noted that the differential between March and September bank-bill futures is 50 basis points. The trader believes that over the coming month longer-dated bill rates will rise relative to the shorter-dated bill rates and, consequently, the spread differential between the two contracts will widen to 100 basis points. To take advantage of this the trader decides to execute a spread trade by buying the March contract and simultaneously selling the September contract. Once the differential widens, the spread trade will be closed, crystallising a profit.

February 10 (spread 50 basis points)

Trader sells 100 March 90–day bank-bill futures at 93.00 (7%) value: $49 151 629.41	Trader buys 100 September 90–day bank-bill futures at 93.50 (6.5%) value: $49 211 271.40

March 10 (spread widens to 100 basis points)

Trader buys 100 March 90–day bank-bill futures at 93.25 (6.75%), value: $49 181 432.33 loss: $29 802.92 net profit $59 931.96	Trader sells 100 September 90-day bank-bill futures at 94.25 (5.7%), value: $49 301 006.28 profit $89 734.88

The trader was therefore able to profit from the change in the spread differential. It was irrelevant whether interest rates rose or fell in absolute terms; the profitability of the trade was contingent on the change (in this case the widening) of the spread between the two contract months.

An intercommodity spread involves buying and selling different futures contracts to take advantage of the relative price changes between the two. A commonly used intercommodity spread is the three-year and ten-year bond futures spread which is often used by bond dealers trading the shape of the yield curve.

Regulation

The futures industry is regulated by the Australian Securities Commission under Chapter 8 of the Corporations Law and by the SFE's business rules. Regulation requirements include licensing of futures brokers, registration of client advisers and segregation of client funds. Regulatory issues relevant to derivatives are discussed in chapter 11.

CHAPTER 3

. . . .

FORWARDS

Derivatives in the form of forward contracts have been used for centuries. Forward trading by written contract is recorded as early as the sixth century BC in Greece, when Thales, an astute philosopher, cornered the olive presses. He contracted, before harvest, to use all the available capacity and then, after a record harvest, forced the olive oil producers to pay higher prices to use his presses. Later, in the Middles Ages, transactions took place using a type of forward delivery document. Used at the European trade fairs, these were initially issued only with a sale of cash commodities between a buyer and a seller; later they evolved into negotiable documents.

Forward contracts, as well as being one of the earliest forms of derivatives, are also one of the simplest. Under a forward contract one party commits to buy and another to sell a specific item at a specific price, for a specific amount and at a date set in the future. The contracts operate like over-the-counter futures contracts. However, unlike futures markets, where contracts are standardised and traded on an exchange, forward contracts are negotiated between two parties, ie, they are 'customised' as to terms and conditions to suit each individual counterparty's business and risk-management needs.

Forward markets exist for a variety of underlying assets and instruments, ranging from the traditional agricultural commodities to gold, currencies and interest rates. For example, in a forward-rate agreement, two counterparties would agree to exchange interest-rate differentials on a notional principal amount at a given future date. A forward contract in gold would involve, say, a gold producer and a bank agreeing to a purchase and sale of gold at some future date, possibly one, three, six or twelve months hence—whatever time-frame is acceptable to the market. (See chapter 7 for a discussion of derivatives techniques used in the gold market.) Or a bank could write a forward foreign exchange contract with a client, agreeing to sell to, or buy from, the client a specific quantity of foreign exchange at a set future date at a price agreed now. Contracts are settled either by calculating net differences or by the exchange of gross amounts. The currency hedge market that developed in Australia in the 1970s, in the days when the 'official' foreign-exchange market was closed to all but trade-related transactions, operated with non-deliverable contracts and the hedge contract was in many respects a forerunner of later forwards and swaps that now fall under the umbrella of 'derivatives'.

Both parties to a forward contract are vulnerable to the risk of default for the life of the contract, so the credit risk created by a forward contract remains until the contract matures. Credit risk dictates that counterparties to forward contracts are generally well-rated companies, banks, financial institutions, institutional investors or government bodies.

FORWARD-RATE AGREEMENTS: DEVELOPMENT AND GROWTH

Before the advent of foward-rate agreements (FRAs), a lender providing fixed-rate funds was locked into the conditions of the loan for the specified term. Many suffered when market rates rose—if they had not covered market risk in some other way—because they were unable to vary their charges. Likewise, a borrower would be disadvantaged when rates fell during the term of a fixed borrowing, or if rates rose before a future known borrowing could be put in place.

FRAs enable interest-rate exposure to be altered. An FRA has greater flexibility than a standardised futures contract in that any starting date and term can be struck. An FRA is similar to a synthetic forward bank-bill purchase or sale. It has also been described as a single-period interest-rate swap (and a swap likened to a string of FRAs). The contract is made at an agreed interest rate, for a specified period, based on an agreed notional principal amount, between any two parties looking to protect themselves against a future movement in interest rates. Principal amounts are not exchanged. Each party's exposure is to the difference between the rate agreed under the FRA and the settlement rate.

The FRA market began in London in 1983 and quickly spread to Australia where it is a large sector of the OTC derivatives markets. FRAs are actively traded in the wholesale market. A survey for AFMA by the Financial Products Research Group showed trading volume for the year to June 1994 was $690 billion, a substantial 40 per cent increase over that of the previous year. This reflected market response to the upward trend in interest rates in 1994 and contrasted sharply with the pattern of the previous year: volume to June 1993, when interest rates were in the trough of the cycle, had been virtually static at $492 billion.

Financial Products' analysis showed that the total number of transactions rose by only 5 per cent but the average size of the transactions increased from around $3 million in 1992/93 to just under $50 million in 1993/94. Within the 1994 growth, the interbank segment represented 51 per cent of the total, down from the previous year's 60 per cent; the level of corporate use of FRAs increased by 75 per cent, from $53 billion to $86 billion, accounting for 13 per cent of the total market volume compared with 11 per cent in 1993.

FRAs have become the principal yield-curve positioning tool for interest-rate speculation. Most activity is in $A FRAs but there is modest volume in $US, deutschmark, sterling and yen-based FRAs. The yen-based FRA market would receive a significant boost if the Japanese authorities allowed their banks to trade FRAs domestically as well as offshore.

Use of FRAs

FRAs can be considered as tailor-made (OTC) futures contracts without the associated constraints of brokerage, margins, standard dates and contract size. FRAs retain the off-balance-sheet advantages of the futures market.

FRAs are chiefly used by professional market operators for trading in-house and hedging and to provide hedging products to investors, companies and governments. An FRA enables borrowers and lenders to lock into future interest rates without exchanging principal amounts of the borrowing or loan. The agreement is struck between a client and a bank or investment bank, which fixes the interest rate to apply to an expected loan or deposit, for an agreed amount, term and date. Neither party in an FRA is committed to lend or borrow the principal amount, so each party's exposure is limited to the difference between the agreed interest rate and the rate that applies when the FRA is settled.

The bank or investment bank calculates the forward rate from an implied yield curve for the period specified. On the agreed future date, the difference between the rate struck under the FRA and the prevailing market rate is settled between client and bank. Where the client has locked in a borrowing rate that proves to be lower than the bank-bill rate at the end of the agreed period, the bank pays the difference to the client, whose effective borrowing rate thus drops to the agreed forward rate; if, on the other hand, the rates set under the FRA prove to be higher than prevailing interest rates, the client pays the difference to the bank or investment bank, and raises its effective borrowing cost to that earlier agreed. Interbank FRAs in Australia are quoted to a maturity of one year, but longer maturities are available. Market convention is that the lender of an FRA is the *offer* and the borrower is the *bid*.

A borrower with an expected three-month borrowing requirement due to start in two months could use an FRA to protect against a possible rise in interest rates before the borrowing is drawn down. This borrower would hedge using a 'two-month against five-month' FRA—this means setting a rate today to apply in two months for a three-month borrowing. Likewise, a lender expecting surplus funds in two months that could be invested for six months could take a 'two-month against eight-month' FRA.

Example: hedging a future borrowing

Aussie Co Pty Ltd plans to draw down $1 million in 90-day bills in three months, and would like to secure a rate today for its future borrowings. Assume:

Bank bills (face value)	$1 000 000
Date 05/04/95	
FRA rate (starting 05/07/95 for 90 days)	11.0 per cent
Actual 90-day rate on 05/07/95	11.5 per cent

Sequence of events:

1 On 05/04/95 Aussie Co enters into an FRA with First Bank.
2 On 05/07/95 the 90–day bank-bill rate, as shown on AAP Reuters page BBSW, is 11.5 per cent.
3 Because that is higher than the rate at which both parties entered the FRA, ie, 11.0 per cent, First Bank must pay the difference to Aussie Co.
4 The settlement amount is equal to the difference between $1 million discounted at 11.0 per cent and $1 million discounted at 11.5 per cent, ie, $1167.22, and is paid by First Bank to Aussie Co.
5 If, on 05/07/95, the 90-day bank-bill rate shown on BBSW were 10.75 per cent, then the settlement amount would be equal to the difference betweeen $1 million discounted at 10.75 per cent and $1 million discounted at 11.0 per cent, being $584.66, and would be paid by Aussie Co to First Bank. (NB: settlement is calculated on a discount, not yield, basis.)

Figure 3.1   Example of a forward-rate agreement

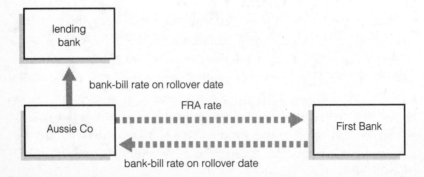

Example: hedging a future investment

1   Aussie Co expects to receive $1 million in three months, which it will invest in a three-month bank bill or certificate of deposit.
2   To protect against a possible fall in interest rates over coming months, before the investment is put in place, Aussie Co sells an FRA, locking in today's interest rate for the future deposit.
3   First Bank is quoting a three-month against six-month FRA at 11.3–11.05 per cent and Aussie Co agrees to a contract rate of 11.05 per cent.
4   If, in three months, the settlement rate is 10.30 per cent, First Bank will settle in favour of Aussie Co and, on FRA settlement date:

Aussie Co buys a $1 million bank bill @ 10.3% (90 days)	$975 231.78
Aussie Co has locked in $1 million @ 11.05% for 90 days on an FRA	$973 476.11
FRA settlement amount	1 755.67

ie, Aussie Co will receive $1755.67
    on settlement of the FRA.

If, in three months, the settlement rate is 11.8 per cent, Aussie Co will settle in favour of First Bank and, on FRA settlement date:

Aussie Co buys $1 million bank bill @ 11.8% (90 days)	$971 726.75
Aussie Co has locked in $1 million @ 11.05% for 90 days on an FRA	973 476.11
FRA settlement amount	1 749.36

ie, Aussie Co will pay First Bank $1749.36
    on settlement of the FRA.

Advantages of FRAs

-   FRAs are flexible, whereas futures contracts are standardised in terms of amount and settlement date, and futures trading concentrates on calendar quarters. FRAs can be tailored to suit the requirements of each borrower or lender (within an ambit two-year period);

- credit risk is limited to the variation in interest rates and not to the full principal amount involved;
- FRAs are settled by exchanging amounts of cash and the principal amounts involved are not carried on the balance sheet for the period hedged;
- administration is simple—FRAs are not traded on an exchange so there is no demand for an initial deposit or margin calls, brokerage or clearing-house fees. Cashflows are therefore more predictable and, with no margins to monitor, accounting costs are minimised;
- market depth. For those dealing out to one year, the futures market provides more liquidity, but FRAs offer greater liquidity out to two years. The narrow spreads quoted on FRAs, for example three–five basis points, reflect the depth of the market, which is able to absorb large parcels. The Australian interbank market in FRAs includes between fifteen and twenty banks while a larger group of around 30 offer the instruments to clients, and several broking firms help to match the different dates sought;
- FRAs enable interest-rate risk to be hedged without making demands on current liquidity;
- FRAs are increasingly being settled under Aussie ISDA (the standard documentation used when trading Australian risk-management products; see 'Learning the Language') and, while they can still be settled under the ABAFRA terms (recommended by the $A FRA working party of banks and merchant banks, operating under the auspices of the Australian Bankers' Association; see 'Learning the Language'), the objective is that ultimately all settlements will be handled under Aussie ISDA;
- settlement of FRAs is against the bank-bill swap reference rate shown daily at 10.10am on AAP Reuters page BBSW. The rate is a midrate, so neither side pays a spread.

Disadvantage

FRAs do suffer from the disadvantage of not operating in a formal market, as do futures, and of carrying a credit risk in a way that futures contracts do not (since the risk in a futures contract is borne by the clearing house which is in turn protected by deposits and margins).

FRA TERMS

broken period	a settlement period that differs in length from that used in fixing the interest settlement rate
buyer/borrower	the party wishing to protect against a rise in interest rates
contract amount	notional sum on which the FRA is based
contract date	the date the FRA is entered into
contract rate	the rate of interest agreed between the parties on contract date
maturity date	the date the settlement period ends
run	period or term of the underlying investment or borrowing, normally 90 or 180 days (a three or six-month run)
settlement date	the date at the start of the period covered by the FRA, when the agreed FRA rate is compared with the BBSW rate
seller/lender	the party wishing to protect against a fall in interest rates
settlement period	the period between the settlement date and maturity date of the FRA
settlement rate	the mean rate quoted by specified reference banks for the relevant period. The settlement rate for $A FRAs is the average bank-bill rate shown on AAP Reuters BBSW page.

FORWARD FOREIGN EXCHANGE

Until December 1983, when the $A was floated and exchange controls removed, foreign-exchange trading was the preserve of the trading banks. Access to forward cover against movements in the exchange rate was restricted to trade-related transactions and, until October 1983, cover had to be taken out within seven days of incurring a currency exposure. The response to these restrictions was the emergence of a currency hedge market which married opposite risks between two parties. A foreign-currency hedge was a contract between two parties where each agreed to pay to the other, on a future date, an adjustment expressed in $A—the adjustment being the difference between the $A equivalent of a specified amount of foreign currency converted at the hedge contract rate agreed at the outset and the $A equivalent of the same foreign currency amount converted at rates prevailing on the settlement date. Currency hedge contracts matched precise amounts of money and settlement dates. No movement of foreign currencies was involved; rather, the market was based on net $A settlements (to avoid physical delivery of foreign currency which would have contravened exchange controls).

The changes in 1983 freed the Australian foreign-exchange market and enabled foreign exchange to be traded by a far wider pool of operators and to be traded using deliverable contracts. A deep and liquid market developed in foreign exchange, trading spot (delivery in two business days) and forward (delivery at a future date which could range from three days to one year hence). Contracts executed for longer than one year are termed medium-term or long-term forwards (MTFX or LTFX). Most activity in the foreign-exchange market reflects speculative interest, particularly at the shorter end of the market, rather than trade and investment. Speculation, arbitrage and professional dealing is behind most of the action, with currencies bought and sold like commodities. The chief participants in foreign exchange are the major banks, investment banks, fund managers, companies, central banks and foreign-exchange brokers. The increase in international investment, and thus in capital flows, has helped feed the volume in foreign-exchange markets.

The foreign-exchange market falls into two sectors, spot and forward. The price at which two foreign currencies change hands is the exchange rate. The spot price for a currency is the exchange rate prevailing for a transaction settled in two business days; settlement for any longer term is forward. The spot rate for the $A against the $US is expressed as, say, 0.7650 which means one $A = 76.50 US cents. However, the quote is more likely to read 0.7650/7655, which gives the bank's buy/sell (bid and offer) rates. The quote indicates that the bank is buying $A and selling $US at 0.7650, and is selling $A and buying $US at 0.7655. The spread between the two is the profit or margin the bank makes if handling both sides of a transaction. A simple rule is that the customer always receives the lower amount, the bank the larger. At 0.7650/7655 $US to the $A, the customer receives 76.50 US cents for every $A sold to the bank, while it *costs* the customer 76.55 US cents to buy one Australian dollar.

Forward markets in foreign exchange developed to suit the needs of borrowers and lenders, importers and exporters, who have to make or receive foreign-currency payments in the future. The chief motives for trading foreign exchange are hedging, (taking cover against unpredictable movements in the exchange rate), speculation or arbitrage. An example of a *hedger* is an importer who has agreed to buy a tractor made in Germany and to pay on delivery in six months; or an exporter who knows it will need to convert proceeds from a sale in Japan in three months; or a borrower who has to repay an overseas borrowing or wants to convert an overseas fundraising into $A.

A trader *arbitraging* different markets or currencies has no inherent foreign-exchange risk that requires covering. The arbi-trager is taking advantage of potential opportunities for profit arising from short-term anomalies in the prices of currencies or in interest rates. Arbitragers are professional traders who have to be quick on their feet because their 'windows of opportunity' open and close quickly. They also need extensive credit lines. *Speculators* accept the possibility of adverse exchange-rate movements in the hope of making a profit. Speculators have no underlying trade transaction.

Forward prices are based on the spot rate of a currency plus or minus a margin. The margin reflects the differential in interest rates between the two countries concerned and varies with the period for which the forward contract is written. The forward rate therefore has two components: the spot rate and the forward points, or margin. An 'outright' forward is the total of the spot rate plus or minus the forward points. A guide to remembering whether to add or deduct the forward points is: if forward points are going from high to low, deduct them from the spot rate; if the forward points are going from low to high, add them to the spot rate.

Say the spot $A/$US rate is	0.7650/7655
(ie, $A1.00 = 76.50/76.55 US cents)	
And the forward margin (2 months) is	24/22
The forward points are moving from high to	
low so deduct to get the outright forward of	0.7626/7633

In the above example the forward value of the $A is less than spot, indicating that the $A is at a forward discount to the $US. This reflects interest-rate differentials. The currency of the country with the higher interest rates trades at a forward discount (forward value below spot) to that of the other; the currency with lower interest rates trades at a forward premium (forward value above spot).

A company or trader wanting to take out forward cover against movements in a foreign currency enters into a forward contract with a bank. For example, an importer wants to fix the rate at which it can buy lira in six months to pay for goods coming from Italy. The bank agrees to sell the lira in six months but in the meantime, to cover itself, the bank may decide to buy the necessary amount of lira in the spot foreign-exchange market and invests it for six months. To fund this purchase the bank would borrow $A for six months and repays that borrowing when the importer pays $A for its lira.

To calculate the forward rate:

The spot rate for $A against lira is	1210/12
(ie, one $A = 1210/12 lira)	
The six-month forward margin is	3/6
The forward points are moving from low to high	
so add to get an outright forward	1213/18

The importing company has eliminated currency risk. It now knows how many $A it will need to buy lira in six months and so can set a price on goods it will be selling.

FOREIGN EXCHANGE (FX) SWAP

An FX swap is a purchase of one currency against another at an initial date and an agreement to reverse the transaction at a future date and at a specified rate. The difference between the exchange rate applying initially and the rate at which the swap is reversed reflects the interest differentials between the two currencies concerned (the forward points). Initially used to extend or match cashflows with the physical delivery of imports or exports, FX swaps have come to be used also as a funding mechanism against short-term borrowings or by the professional market to speculate on interest-rate movements.

An FX swap differs from a cross-currency swap which involves the exchange of interest payments between counterparties (see chapter 4).

Foreign-exchange markets are discussed in detail in *FOREX—The Techniques of Foreign Exchange*, by Edna Carew and Will Slatyer and *Foreign Exchange Management* by Allan, Elstone, Lock & Valentine, both published by Allen & Unwin.

CHAPTER 4

....

SWAPS

A swap is an over-the-counter (OTC) contract between two parties, with each agreeing to exchange his or her respective obligations. Swaps can be used to arbitrage capital markets to reduce the cost of funds, to increase returns by changing the interest stream of an underlying asset or to eliminate the risks involved in funding fixed-rate or long-term assets with floating-rate or short-term funds.

DEVELOPMENT AND GROWTH

Before the advent of swaps, a lender providing fixed-rate term funds was locked into the conditions of the loan for the specified term. Many suffered when market rates rose (if market risk had not been covered in some way) because they were unable to vary their charges. Credit-tiering resulted in rigidities. For example, governments would have access to fixed-interest markets where, as long-term borrowers, they preferred predictable interest costs. At the other end of the spectrum would be companies which, with the exception of top-class credits, could not raise fixed-term funds because those lending to them preferred to provide floating-rate finance. In between were the banks, which by and large lent at floating rates because this matched the mostly floating-rate nature of their borrowings, and the institutions, which borrowed long-term fixed-rate funds as a counterpart to their long-term investments.

Swaps brought a way to manage these cashflows more flexibly. Swaps enable a state government borrower, for example, to raise floating-rate debt at a cheaper rate than through traditional sources; at the same time they provide companies with access to fixed-rate finance—if that is what better suits each party's cashflow. The determining factor is that traders and company treasurers—anyone managing cashflows—cannot afford to ignore the risks associated with funding fixed assets with floating-rate liabilities, or $A liabilities with yen assets. Such practices could involve opportunity costs, or worse.

Swap techniques have been used increasingly in Australia since the mid-1980s. The two main categories are interest-rate swaps and currency swaps, with interest-rate swaps by far the larger. The development of the swaps market was a response to restrictions on international capital flows (and was also fuelled by arguments about comparative advantage, domestically and internationally). The search for a mechanism to bypass these restrictions led to the emergence of currency swaps.

Currency swaps evolved from the parallel and back-to-back loans popular in the late 1960s and 1970s. In the case of parallel loans, these were structured through, say, a UK company lending sterling, for a fixed term and at a fixed rate, to the UK subisidiary of, say, a US company. Across the Atlantic, the US company would lend an equivalent amount of $US for the same maturity to the US subsidiary of the UK company. This transaction avoided any cross-border movement of funds and so avoided exchange controls. According to Satyajit Das in *Swap Financing*, this led to the first currency swap in 1976, arranged by Continental Illinois and Goldman Sachs for a Dutch company and a British company and involving guilders and sterling. The World Bank gave a boost to the use of swaps when it entered into a swap agreement in 1981 with IBM which enabled IBM to pay the World Bank's $US obligations while the World Bank serviced IBM's obligations in Swiss francs and deutschmarks. In *Swap Financing*, Das writes that the first interest-rate swaps were also arranged in 1981, initially between Citibank and Continental Illinois. The first swap in Australia was transacted in 1983 between the Commonwealth Bank and AIDC. Just over a decade later, in the year to June 1994, the total volume of swaps dealt was $A274 billion, an increase of 41 per cent over the previous year's $A195 billion, according to a survey carried out for the Australian Financial Markets Association (AFMA) by Financial Products Research Group.

Although the currency swap came first, the dominant type of swap used in the markets is the interest-rate swap, which grew out of the earlier currency transactions. This reflects two factors: most borrowers raise funds in their own currency, and interest-rate swaps involve less of a credit risk than currency swaps because, with interest-rate swaps, there is no exchange of principal amounts. The basic concept of a swap remains fairly simple but details can become complex. In its most straightforward form, a plain vanilla/generic swap involves two parties exchanging interest payments for a certain period; one pays floating rate, the other fixed rate and the settlement is for the net difference between the two interest costs.

A further stage in the development of swaps came with eurobond credit arbitrage. While the euromarkets helped drive swaps, they did not necessarily underpin the swaps market which went on to develop a maturity of its own. However, the $A eurobond market flourished during the mid-1980s because of the wide interest-rate differentials between the Australian and European currencies which attracted substantial interest from retail investors in Germany, Belgium and the Netherlands.

Australian semi-government borrowers, such as NSW TCorp and QTC (Queensland Treasury Corporation), provided a major boost to the swaps market, especially in the late 1980s when the volume of commonwealth government bonds was declining as the federal government ran budget surpluses. The semi-government—also known as state-government—borrowers grouped their debt into big, liquid lines of 'hot stocks' which were actively traded. The semis became major users of the swaps market as part of their liability and asset management. The consolidation of debt into hot stocks, and active fee-based stock-lending programs (which improve the market-makers' ability to provide liquidity) have led to semi-government bonds being increasingly used as benchmarks for pricing.

The swaps market was also fuelled by the reverse dual-currency bonds of the 1980s. These bonds were very popular with borrowers, mostly European banks, which issued bonds with a $A coupon and a yen principal. Such was their popularity in 1990 that a survey by the International Swap Dealers Association (ISDA, now International Swaps and Derivatives Association) reported that more than 60 per cent of $A currency swaps business was $A/yen. The largest such transaction was carried out by the Kingdom of Denmark, for $120 billion yen. Dual-currency bonds generated a large volume of swap deals before narrowing interest-rate differentials and changed currency levels removed much of the appeal.

The most recent stage in the swaps market came with the issuing of Matilda bonds, global $A bonds issued by international borrowers such as the European Investment Bank.

TYPES OF SWAPS

Interest-rate swaps

Interest-rate swaps form the largest category, accounting for $177 billion out of a total of $274 billion in $A interest-rate and cross-currency swaps executed in the year to June 1994.

An interest-rate swap is a contract between two parties under which they agree to exchange interest payments. Generally, this involves the exchange of fixed-interest payments for floating-interest payments, or *vice versa*. An important distinction is that there is no exchange of principal amounts under an interest-rate swap because they are equal and in the same currency. Payment of fixed and floating-rate obligations are generally made on the same day and are settled by calculating and paying the cash difference, which reduces the credit exposure between counterparties and simplifies administration.

The driving feature that makes a swap worthwhile is one party's relative credit advantage in a particular market, ie, it can borrow fairly easily in a number of markets but at especially favourable rates in one. The swap technique enables each party to the transaction to borrow in the market where it achieves the best terms and then exchange the conditions of its borrowings to achieve a lower cost and the desired interest-rate profile.

An example: Aussie Co has taken on a five-year loan on which it pays 1 per cent over the bank-bill rate and on which it has to make semi-annual interest payments to the lending bank. Aussie Co would like to gain access to fixed-rate borrowings through a swap. AAA government authority can borrow fixed for five years at 10 per cent, giving it a comparative advantage of at least 2 per cent over Aussie Co in the fixed-rate market. However, AAA government authority has a need for floating-rate funds, which it can borrow, at worst, at the bank-bill rate plus 0.05 per cent (but it cannot raise floating-rate funds for the term it wants). Using an intermediary, Aussie Co and AAA government authority swap their interest payments in a way that provides Aussie Co with a swapped cost of 11.5 per cent, or 0.5 per cent less than the 12 per cent it could achieve itself in the fixed-rate market, and AAA government authority with bank bill less 0.15–25 per cent, about 0.20–0.30 per cent below the rate it would have had to pay had it directly tapped the floating-rate market. Timing is important in achieving the desired swap rate. Typically, the swap would be organised through an intermediary, such as a bank or investment bank. State borrowers have a list of banks which they regard as acceptable swaps counterparties from the point of view of credit and expertise. Diagrammatically and assuming a bank-bill rate of 8 per cent:

Figure 4.1 Example of an interest-rate swap

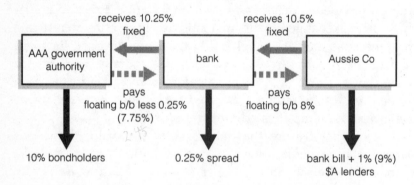

Swaps are generally organised and traded in market parcels of between $10 and $30 million, regardless of their maturity. A professional swaps player's preference is for a parcel of $20 million, with $10 million regarded as a minimum (otherwise a premium might be charged for illiquidity). Companies usually approach the swaps market to pay fixed and receive floating, to generate synthetic fixed-rate funding, while state borrowers, which mostly issue fixed-interest debt, use swaps to receive fixed and pay floating, to raise synthetic floating-rate funding more cheaply than would be available from traditional sources.

Swaps involving an exchange of fixed for floating rates, with interest calculated in arrears, usually pay interest quarterly or semi-annually. When the interest payment on a swap is calculated using the formula for a discounted bill of exchange, ie, the discount or 'up-front' method, the swap is known as a *discounted swap*. The formula used when settling a discounted swap is the same as that used for a forward-rate agreement.

Swaps transacted on an exchange-for-physical (EFP) basis now account for around 90 per cent of interbank trading. An EFP is the simultaneous purchase and sale of a physical instrument (including swaps) with a corresponding opposite futures contract taken out. This leaves both parties with a hedged position which can be managed at each's discretion.

Pricing

Interest-rate swaps are generally priced relative to an underlying physical instrument, usually a commonwealth or state bond or a eurobond, or, in the case of shorter swaps—say, up to two years in maturity—off a bond/bill futures strip (a continuous string of sequential contracts created by buying or selling futures). A considerable volume of swaps during the 1980s was based on the then popular euro-$A bonds, or euro-Aussies. As with other interest rates and prices, swap prices are influenced by supply and demand in the market, with the demand for, and supply of, fixed-rate money determining the swap rate. Indicative rates for swaps are displayed on screens and are also published in the daily press.

Types of interest-rate swap

The following are variations of the interest-rate swap. Complex versions can be achieved by adding 'exotics' to a standard or 'vanilla' product.

Forward swaps start from a date set in the future. For example, a borrower with a debt due to start in three months' time can lock in a fixed rate now instead of waiting until the borrowing is drawn down. Forward swaps could go out as far as a bank's credit risk and policy will allow, say planning a six-year swap to start four years hence.

Zero-coupon swaps are those in which the fixed-interest payment due is paid out as a lump sum, in the form of a 'bullet' payment, when the swap matures.

Amortised and escalating swaps involve a swap where a single swap rate applies to a principal which increases (with an escalating swap, also known as *accreting* swap) or decreases (with an amortised swap) over time.

Basis swaps differ from regular swaps in that they involve an exchange of two different floating interest rates, or fixed-rate for fixed-rate funds instead of the conventional fixed-rate for floating-rate funds. A basis swap involves different time periods; for example, a company might want to receive floating-rate payments structured on a 90-day rollover and make floating-rate payments on a 180-day rollover.

Non-par swaps are swaps where the fixed and floating rates are based on a non-market interest rate with appropriate cash adjustments.

Rollercoaster swaps involve a variation of the principal or the coupon during the life of the swap.

Currency swaps

Cross-currency-and-interest-rate swaps, known as currency swaps, where each side is denominated in a different currency, involve an exchange of the principal amounts, at an agreed exchange rate, as well as an exchange of interest payments in the two different currencies. (This differs from the generic 'FX' swap which is purely a purchase and sale, and, at a pre-agreed rate, a subsequent sale and repurchase of currency on maturity. The interest differential in this case is handled by adding the forward points to, or subtracting them from, the contract price on maturity.) With currency swaps the interest differential is handled through mutual exchange of interest flows and not through the forward points. Credit risk is a greater issue with

Figure 4.2   Example of a currency swap

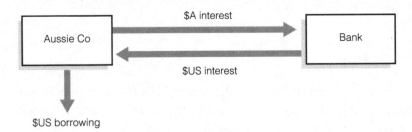

currency swaps because principal amounts are swapped and a foreign-exchange exposure incurred. Many currency swaps are structured using euro–$A bonds and other euromarket issues. These swaps may be on a fixed-to-fixed, fixed-to-floating, or floating-to-floating interest-rate basis. They are also known as currency-and-interest-rate swaps.

Commodity swaps

Commodity swaps have emerged as risk-management tools for the 1990s, propelled by the same factors that drove the popularity of currency and interest-rate swaps: volatility and uncertainty—this time, volatility and uncertainty in the price of, say, oil, gold, wool, wheat or cotton. So far, most Australian activity has been in oil swaps; gold, aluminium and copper tend to be traded forward rather than swapped. The bulk of commodity swaps volume is handled overseas, although Australian consumers (refiners and those with big transport costs), do hedge their oil costs. Airlines have been major users of oil swaps. A commodity swap enables a producer to fix future revenues at a specified level and, on the other side, enables a consumer to set future costs. Each gives up any increased income or reduced costs should prices move in his or her favour. Commodity swaps are similar in structure to the earlier financial swap. Given that the two parties to a commodity swap, producer and consumer, through an intermediary, exchange a stream of payments (fixed for floating cashflow) with no exchange of principal, a commodity swap is more like an interest-rate swap than a currency swap. A bank or investment bank acts as intermediary, bringing the two parties together and taking a spread between payments for bearing the credit risk of each. (See chapter 7.)

Equity swaps

Equity swaps would typically be used by a fund manager, institutional equity manager or a company to protect the price risk of an equity portfolio. An organisation with a diversified share portfolio could use an equity swap to convert an unpredictable return on shares into a fixed income or a return based on a floating interest-rate indicator. Equity swaps, discussed in chapter 6, are more common in the US and Europe but increasing in use in Australia. They share the characteristics of a conventional swap such as notional principal, specified term, predetermined payments made at intervals, a fixed rate (swap coupon) and an exchange of income streams by the parties to the swap.

Macroeconomic swaps

Macroeconomic swaps are designed to hedge against macroeconomic risk, ie, whereas an interest-rate swap provides protection against a specific risk—interest-rate risk—a macroeconomic swap provides protection against general business risk such as a downturn in economic activity. Macroeconomic swaps were first proposed in 1991 in the US by Marshall, Bansal, Herbst and Tucker as tools for companies wishing to hedge against business-cycle risk. Two essential ingredients are a suitable macroeconomic index, such as the CPI (consumer price index) or GDP (gross domestic product) and an adequate degree of correlation between the index and the hedging company's earnings. An example of a macroeconomic swap would be a fixed-for-floating swap where the floating-leg payment is based on a macroeconomic index or a floating-for-floating swap in which one leg is pegged to a macroeconomic index and the other to a floating rate of interest. Macroeconomic swaps are like conventional swaps in that they comprise a notional principal, swap coupon (fixed rate), regular payments and specified term.

SWAPS MARKET PARTICIPANTS

Derivatives such as swaps, options and FRAs involve two main categories of participants—sellers of, or dealers in, the products (intermediaries such as banks and investment banks) and end-users, which covers a wide range including overseas investors, companies, fund managers and state government borrowers.

Banks and investment banks market swaps to corporate clients who want to improve their risk-management techniques. These intermediaries play an active role in organising swaps, identifying organisations with offsetting needs, arranging the different forms of financing, negotiating terms, organising documentation and watching market movements to find the right moment at which to execute a deal. Good timing is important in swaps transactions because even a small movement in a currency or interest rate can make a difference to the fixed swap rate, which is the important number in the transaction.

The intermediaries, usually banks, also have a 'client' in their own internal asset and liability management needs. Much business, though, centres on structuring swaps to suit clients. Banks use swaps and other derivatives to manage the interest-rate risks in their own products, for example the offer of a capped or fixed housing loan to a retail borrower. Until recently, retail customers had virtually no access to derivatives but they can benefit from them because derivatives enable the bank to package products and to manage its liabilities more efficiently and to provide a wider choice to customers.

By using swaps, an end-user transfers performance (market) risk (but not the underlying position) to the provider (intermediary) who, in return, earns a spread or margin. End-users enter the swaps market for a number of reasons: to achieve a lower cost of funds or higher returns, to hedge an interest-rate or currency exposure or to improve asset or liability management.

In addition, there is an active broker market in swaps, with brokers acting as agent and earning brokerage for finding the best price. Brokers handle a sizeable volume of interbank business; however, a bank would not see a corporate deal through a broker because that would involve a weakening of the bank–client relationship on which the bank wants to build.

RISKS ASSOCIATED WITH SWAPS

Given the flow of supply and demand, it is unlikely that swaps held by the principals exactly offset each other, so the principals are exposed to various types of market risk; they would take steps to hedge such risk. All market prices move according to supply and demand and the swaps market is no exception. A principal taking on a swap could hedge against the underlying instrument, although such a decision would depend on the structure of his or her swaps book. A principal can also 'warehouse' a swap until an opposite deal is found.

As with other derivatives, swaps do not present new forms of risk; they involve risks with which traders are well familiar, such as those associated with credit, market, liquidity and documentation. Interest-rate swaps involve a credit risk which reflects the ability or otherwise of each counterparty to make payments owed under the swaps agreement. (This credit risk is less than would be the case with an outright loan because, should a default occur, the counterparty is not exposed to loss of the principal amount.) The payments involve the outlay or receipt of the net differences between the fixed and floating rate. Because swaps carry a credit risk, a swap obligation cannot be assigned to another party without the consent of the first counterparty.

Outright risk occurs when a swaps trader is not completely square (balanced) but has some exposure to a particular level of interest rates or change in the slope of the yield curve.

Basis risk involves the risk of a movement between the swap and the product used to hedge it.

Swaps are now managed as warehouses of future cashflows and the price risk of each net future cashflow is hedged.

CHAPTER 5

· · · · · · · · · · · · ·

OPTIONS

DEVELOPMENT AND GROWTH

Options have developed in two broad categories: over-the-counter (OTC) and exchange-traded options (ETOs). OTC options are tailored by banks and investment banks to suit the needs of their clients. Exchange-traded options are available on ASX Derivatives, a division of the Australian Stock Exchange (ASX), which offers a range of options over shares, and on the Sydney Futures Exchange (options over futures contracts). Options have become increasingly popular in recent years as a risk-management tool. While very much a product of the 1980s and 1990s, options are by no means a purely recent innovation; evidence of option contracts dates from at least the Middle Ages and, in the seventeenth century, options were traded on exchanges in Holland (over tulips) and in the UK.

The meteoric growth in OTC options in 1987 and 1988 stabilised in the early 1990s. In the year to June 1994, the volume of interest-rate options dealt rose by 6 per cent to $67 billion, according to the Australian Financial Market Report prepared for AFMA by the Financial Products Research Group Pty Ltd. The survey reviewed three types of options: bond options, caps and floors, and swaptions. The volume of bond options was down by slightly more than 6 per cent to $28 billion while the volume of caps and floors rose by 15 per cent to $33 billion and the volume of swaptions also rose, by 20 per cent to $6 billion. The survey's review of currency options showed a drop of 30 per cent for the year to June 1994, to $US116 billion, setting the currency options market back to levels seen in 1990–92. (The survey noted that the volume of currency options dealt in 1993/94 was affected by the shift of at least one major participant from onshore to offshore price-making, making year-on-year comparisons difficult.)

While the volume of options written is lower than that of swaps, it is options that are said to have the most potential for further growth because of the limited risk for option buyers. When purchasing an option, the buyer pays a premium at the outset for the right to hold the option and this represents the maximum loss the buyer can incur, irrespective of the subsequent trend in market prices. On the other side, the option writer (grantor or seller) carries potentially unlimited risk while the writer's profit is limited to the premium received.

Options are chiefly used either to hedge or to produce income. The initial spurt in growth in OTC options came in bond options, caps and floors. Bond options have been popular despite having an entry price rarely viewed as cheap. Banks were the first to sell over-the-counter bond options, then fund managers realised they too could sell the options and reap an improved return. This gave the options market a further boost. The appeal of over-the-counter (OTC) options, tailored to specific stocks, lies in their ability to provide a more precise match-out for risk.

Exchange-traded options, launched as options over shares in 1976 on what was then the Australian Options Market (now ASX Derivatives) and introduced in their present form on the Sydney Futures Exchange (SFE) in 1985, have recorded enormous growth. SFE options (options on futures contracts) recorded a 31.6 per cent rise in 1994 over volumes in 1993, trading 3.1 million contracts compared with 2.4 million. Average daily volume traded in SFE options was 12 324 in 1994 compared with 9254 in 1993, showing an increase of 33.2 per cent. Trading in options on ASX Derivatives also climbed with the market's average daily business volume in 1994 coming in at 40 500 contracts compared with 37 300 in 1993, a rise of 8.58 per cent.

OPTION TERMINOLOGY

Options can be either *puts* or *calls*. A put option gives the buyer, in return for paying a premium, the right, but not the obligation, to sell at a specific rate or price; a call option gives the buyer, in return for paying a premium, the right, but not the obligation, to buy at a specific rate or price. The *strike* or *exercise* price of an option is the price at which an option buyer may exercise his or her right to buy or sell the underlying asset over which the option was written.

Options are further defined as *in-the-money, at-the-money* and *out-of-the-money*. A strike price is in-the-money if the option can be exercised at a profit at that time. For example, a call option (an option to buy) is in-the-money when the strike price is below the prevailing rate or price of the relevant obligation. The opposite of in-the-money is out-of-the-money. A put option (an option to sell) is out-of-the-money if the strike price is below the prevailing rate or price. An option is at-the-money if the current strike price is the same as the prevailing market price.

The cost of an option is known as the *premium*. From the point of view of an option buyer, a premium is similar to a one-off insurance premium. For the option writer or seller, the premium is the reward for taking the risk in granting/selling the right conveyed by the option. A high premium is in the grantor's interest but a grantor is constrained from overcharging by competition from other grantors and the level of demand from takers.

Another influence on the level of an option premium is the *intrinsic value* of an option. This is the amount by which an option is in-the-money. By definition, an out-of-the-money option has no intrinsic value, but it is still bought because, from a hedger's point of view, it provides some protection (it has a time value). The premium asked for an out-of-the-money option varies depending on how far the strike price is from the market price. The further an option is out-of-the-money, the cheaper its premium will be, because it is less likely to expire in-the-money or be exercised.

A deep in-the-money option costs more than an at-the-money option because it has an intrinsic value and is more likely to expire in-the-money, or be exercised. Put premiums move in the opposite direction to call premiums. If a call option is in-the-money, then a put option (over the same underlying instrument and at the same strike price) is out-of-the-money.

The longer the life of an option, the longer the period for which the grantor has to carry a risk, so the grantor demands a higher premium. Further, the more volatile the price of the underlying asset, the more risk the grantor is being asked to assume, so the grantor will want a higher reward in the form of a higher premium. Volatile prices also tend to increase the likelihood of an option being exercised, which further influences a grantor to demand a higher premium. Options that are not exercised become worthless and simply expire. Option traders talk of an option having an *expiry*, rather than maturity, date.

Table 5.1 illustrates the effect of volatility on an option. Put and call option premiums rise when volatility increases. Table 5.2 illustrates the effect of the passage of time on an option. Put and call premiums decline in line with the time to expiry.

PRICING AN OPTION

Pricing is critical with options. The option price (premium) takes into account two features, the intrinsic value and the time value of the option. The intrinsic value is the profit available to the option holder if the option were immediately exercised, ie, the difference between the market value of the underlying asset or instrument and the exercise price of the option. The time value of an option represents the chance that the price of the under-lying asset (eg, bond, currency, futures contract, share or commodity) will move in a favourable direction, causing the option to become in-the-money; time value declines as the option approaches its expiry date.

There are six key influences on the option premium:

- the strike price;
- the price of the underlying asset or instrument;
- the time to expiry of the option;
- market volatility in the underlying asset or instrument;
- interest rates; and
- market expectations.

Table 5.1   Effect of volatility

SFE All Ordinaries SPI Futures
Futures price: 2141. Days to expiry: 60

Volatility	Option premium (2150 call)	Option premium (2150 put)
10%	30.4	39.4
15%	48.5	57.5
20%	65.0	74.0
25%	82.3	91.3

Table 5.2   Effect of time

SFE All Ordinaries SPI Futures
Futures price: 2014. Volatility: 16.5%

Days to expiry	2000 call	2000 put
150	91.8	77.8
90	72.8	58.8
60	60.8	46.8
10	16.1	2.1

A number of formulas are used for pricing options. Most European options pricings, however, are derived from the Black–Scholes pricing model. (A European option is one that can be exercised only on its expiry date. An American option can be exercised at any time up to and including the expiry date.) Developed in the early 1970s by two US economists, Fischer Black and Myron Scholes, the model highlighted the potential of options for limiting risk. Computers have played a vital role in the proliferation of option-pricing models, with systems available as 'off-the-shelf' purchases for those who do not want to develop their own.

The valuation of option premiums is of interest both to the grantor (seller) and to the buyer. Those choosing to ignore the calculations and make judgments about market forces do so at considerable risk. On the other side, the hedger who takes or buys options generally merely takes a view about the cost of the premium and whether it is affordable as part of an overall hedging strategy. The more sophisticated hedger trades the market regularly, using options and futures, structures trading strategies and monitors actual, not just implied, premium values.

EXCHANGE-TRADED OPTIONS

ASX Derivatives: options over equities

ASX Derivatives dates from February 1976 when it was launched under the auspices of the Australian Stock Exchange as the Australian Options Market, the first exchange-traded options market outside the US. Widely used by retail investors, the market provides a formal market-place for trading put and call options on a selected list of actively traded equities. Call options, introduced with great success in 1976, were followed in 1982 by put options. Equity options are available in two types: *company-generated* options, which are issued by companies to raise funds, and *exchange-traded* options (ETOs) which are created between investors on the trading floor of the options market (the relevant company is not a party to the contract). ETOs deal in options over existing shares and so do not add to a company's share capital.

In June 1994, the top ten stocks, measured by option contracts traded on the ASX Derivatives were: Fosters, BHP, News Corporation, MIM, Western Mining, National Australia Bank, ANZ, Westpac, CRA and Ampolex. ASX Derivatives also offers a popular cash-settled option over the Twenty Leaders index (TLX) which contains twenty of the most popular stocks. This enables investors to take a view on the 'blue-chip' market in general. TLX is a capitalisation-weighted share price index calculated by the Australian Stock Exchange. Stocks included are selected on the basis of market capitalisation and turnover, and the extent to which they represent a range of Australian economic activity.

Equity derivatives traded on ASX Derivatives are discussed in chapter 6.

Sydney Futures Exchange: options over futures contracts

Options traded on an exchange are known as exchange-traded options (ETOs). The prices of the ETOs traded on the Sydney Futures Exchange (SFE) are negotiated by open outcry on the floor of the exchange in the normal course of trading and are displayed on dealers' screens in the same way as futures market prices. Options have been available on futures contracts traded at the SFE since 1982 when they were first introduced over the bank-bill and $US futures contracts. These early options were non-transferable, ie, the option could not be resold or repurchased during its life; it could only be exercised or abandoned. Since 1985 an exchange-traded options market has existed on the SFE, allowing option-holders to trade out of the options if they choose, thus providing greater flexibility. ETOs have shown consistent growth in volume traded, particularly the options over the SFE's two government bond contracts and, at times, options over the share-price index (SPI) futures contract. They have increased in popularity because they can offer a low-risk—in fact a maximum-known-risk—strategy (in the case of bought options, ie, bought puts or bought calls). Both buyers and sellers of options on the SFE are margined. In effect, though, the holder of an option to buy (a long option holder) is still limited in outlay to the cost of the premium; margin calls can absorb no more than the premium. The seller (short option holder), though, faces an open-ended potential for loss—effectively, he or she holds an equivalent exposure to holding a bought or sold futures contract.

Futures options have been promoted as the best method of limiting risk, particularly if a trader is working with a small amount of capital. Options can be excellent insurance for the buyer; they provide a cushion for a known cost and offer an unlimited potential for gain. The option seller is exposed to the greater risk and, in the absence of an existing offsetting position, would take steps to hedge. Whereas a futures contract is a binding obligation which can only be terminated by closing out, an option buyer is not compelled to exercise the option. If the buyer does not exercise the option, his or her outlay is limited to the premium paid to the grantor, plus brokerage.

In the case of options traded on the Sydney Futures Exchange, the option taker pays a premium for the right to buy or sell a futures contract at an agreed strike price. The buyer can exercise the option at the strike price at any time before the expiry date, irrespective of the level of the futures price. If the market moves in the forecast direction, the buyer may exercise the option and trade the opposite side on the futures market to secure a profit. Alternatively, the buyer may elect to sell the option at the new higher premium and realise a profit in this way. The grantor of an option takes the opposite view to the buyer and is in a riskier position. Grantors are typically professional traders, large institutions or companies familiar with the physical market of the commodity on which the option is based, as well as with the futures market. To offset the risk, which crystallises when an option is exercised, the grantor—who in any case receives a premium—may take a position in the futures market opposite to the option which has been granted.

Flexible options, launched on the Chicago Board Options Exchange in 1993, are under consideration at the SFE. Flexible options combine the versatility of an over-the-counter option with the security of an exchange-traded product. With exchange-traded flex options counterparty risk—a significant concern on the OTC markets—is eliminated. Unlike conventional exchange-traded options a flex option does not carry a standard strike price and expiry date but can be tailored to suit individual hedging requirements.

OVER-THE-COUNTER OPTIONS

Over-the-counter (OTC) options are customised, that is, privately negotiated and tailored to suit each client. Within the OTC category of options come variations such as caps, floors, collars and swaptions. Caps, floors and collars are usually designed by a bank or investment bank for a client but banks and investment banks also write options for their own interest-rate risk management.

A *cap* (put option) is the maximum rate a borrower will be required to pay for funds. By placing a ceiling on interest rates, it provides the borrower with a form of protection or insurance against rate movements. A *floor* (call option), on the other hand, guarantees a minimum rate of return by providing protection against falls in interest rates. In both cases, investors are free to benefit from favourable movements in interest rates by simply abandoning the option and forsaking the premium paid. *Collars*, also known as tunnels or cyclinders, set both minimum and maximum rates beyond which the borrower's interest costs will not move. Because collars have the effect of locking a borrower into an interest-rate band, they involve smaller premiums; they can also be designed as zero-cost collars, with the premium paid equal to the premium received. Demand for caps and collars is likely to increase when traders believe that the interest-rate cycle has bottomed. Caps and floors are quoted out to five years and are generally fairly liquid out to three years.

Interest-rate options, caps and floors

Options are available over a number of financial instruments but most commonly, in the case of interest-rate options, over commonwealth and state government bonds and bank bills. An interest-rate option gives the buyer, in return for paying a premium, the right, but not the obligation, to borrow or lend at a predetermined rate. For example, a borrower wishing to limit interest costs buys a put option (cap) at a strike price of, say, 8.5 per cent. That borrower has the right, but not the obligation, to borrow at 8.5 per cent and has paid a premium for that right to the grantor (writer) of the option. The borrower has effectively bought insurance. The day arrives when the borrower has to decide whether to draw down bank bills under the borrowing facility: if interest rates are above 8.5 per cent the borrower would exercise the option to borrow at the specified strike price of 8.5 per cent; if rates were below 8.5 per cent the borrower does not need the option and so does not exercise it. A floor provides the opposite to a cap, ie, a level below which a lender or investor's rate cannot fall.

Currency options

Currency options give the option holder, in return for paying a premium, the right, but not the obligation, to buy or sell a specified amount of a foreign currency through a spot foreign-exchange transaction at some future date. Options are available over a wide range of currencies but are used mostly over the major trading currencies—$A, $US, deutschmark, yen, sterling

and $NZ. Currency options are sold by banks to a mix of
end-users in which the big exporting companies and mining
companies are predominant. Exporters and fund managers use
currency options, as do importers, although to a lesser extent.
While normally considered buyers, end-users do have the choice
of buying or granting currency options. As grantors they are
exposed to greater risk but, provided they fully grasp how
options work, have the chance to gross up their returns (as is
the case with, say, fund managers and interest-rate options).
Currency options turned in significant growth in the early 1990s,
grew by 47 per cent in the year to June 1993 but, as the Financial
Products Research Group's survey showed, fell by 30 per cent
in the year to June 1994. Lower volumes were reported by all
counterparties except offshore corporates. Both local corporate
and interbank activity recorded a fall of around 40 per cent.
There is very little retail interest in currency options.

Options over commodities

Commodity options, such as those over oil, gold, base metals
and soft commodities, are used by producers and consumers.
(See chapter 7.)

Macroeconomic options

Like macroeconomic swaps, these instruments offer an opportunity to cushion the impact of an economic downturn on
corporate profits and government tax revenues. First proposed
in the US in 1991 by Marshall, Bansal, Herbst and Tucker,
macroeconomic options enable a company to protect its cashflow
and profits from fluctuations in the level of economic activity.
However, the ability to use macroeconomic options assumes the
existence of a reliable index that can be used as a benchmark
and requires a good degree of correlation between the benchmark and the end-user's revenues. In other aspects, such as the
payment of an upfront premium, macroeconomic options
function in the same way as conventional over-the-counter
options.

SWAPTION

A *swaption* is an option over a swap. It gives the buyer the right to enter into a swap at some future date, but imposes no obligation on the buyer to do so. Growth in swaptions has been slower than that of, say, swaps and options. The small size of the swaptions market has been attributed to the discouragingly complicated pricing models used. Caps and floors offer similar protection and are easier to price and to market. An example: Aussie Co is tendering on a project and, if successful, will require fixed-rate debt for five years. Aussie Co will not know for two months whether its bid is successful; however, the five-year swap rates are attractive now. To ensure that it does not miss the desired swap level, Aussie Co buys an option to pay fixed-rate debt at today's strike price, with the option exercisable at the end of the tender period.

Swaptions include the credit risk of an option and that of, say, a five-year swap; a large number of swaptions are transacted on a cash basis to avoid the credit risk, ie, when the option expires and is in-the-money, the parties to the agreement decide to cash-settle rather than enter the swap.

WHO USES OPTIONS?

Financial institutions use both OTC and exchange-traded options; corporates and a broad range of users tap the OTC market and the small player uses exchange-traded options.

Most OTC option business falls into two groups—that generated by institutional holders of bonds and transactions by state borrowers with big portfolios of fixed-interest, fixed-term debt. The market is highly client-driven, particularly by the demands of the state authorities and fund managers. Clients shop for the most competitive premiums, and most have a good idea of where the price level should be. Brokers add to activity levels, ringing around the market on behalf of potential participants. Brokers are also an additional source of information about prices. Fund managers tend to approach the market directly themselves, rather than have a broker chase a price for them.

The OTC bond options market is dominated by professional, wholesale-market players; it does not cater for the small retail trader. Nor are corporates major players in bond options; corporates prefer caps and swaps, which better suit their funding needs (generally short-term, three years and less). Banks and investment banks are active in a small interbank market in options, making prices to each other and running portfolios of options over various instruments. Most transactions in options represent hedging or portfolio management; the remainder, possibly 10 or 20 per cent of activity, represents trading and speculation, and most of that takes place in the exchange-traded options traded on the Sydney Futures Exchange.

RUNNING AN OPTIONS PORTFOLIO: OPTION SENSITIVITIES

Banks and investment banks running options portfolios operate with overall trading limits and limits applying to each counterparty with whom they deal. These limits are set by management. Option books are closely monitored and reports made of trading and positions at the end of each day. Option traders have to be alert to the fact that their hedge positions change with a change in any of the factors affecting the market value of the option, a feature known as *delta*, ie, the expected change in the option price for a given change in the price of the underlying asset or instrument, expressed as a decimal fraction of that change. The option trader has to run through the positions held and identify the exposures to determine what would happen if the market were to rally or dip. Many option books are revalued and rehedged daily to take account of volatility (a significant risk). Option traders must also be aware of funding rates; a trader might execute an options deal and buy stock to hedge it, and must take into account the cost of funding the stock. Another important factor is *theta*, which measures the effect of time on the value of an option (a bought option decreases in value, as it gets closer to expiry date). Theta can be shown by the expected change in the option price in cents per day or, more relevantly, in the value of the option contract in dollars per day.

Gamma measures the rate of change in delta; gamma shows how quickly the risk profile of an option will change when the price of the underlying changes, ie, the sensitivity of the hedged position to price movements in the underlying asset or instrument and thus what hedging is required. *Vega,* (also known as *kappa*), measures the change in the option price given a change in volatility of the underlying asset or instrument and *rho* (also known as *iota*) is the sensitivity of an option price to a change in funding costs (interest rates). Like theta, this can be shown by a change in the option price in cents for each 1 per cent change in rates, or a change in the value of the option contract for a 1 per cent change in interest rates.

Banks, investment banks and others running a portfolio of options use computers to monitor the associated risks. Computer reports would show the position of each option held over a specific underlying instrument, giving its position in the prevailing market and how that would be affected by a rise or fall in interest rates, a change in volatility, a change in the number of days until the option's expiry and, of course, a change in the price of the underlying instrument. Computer reports break the portfolio down into the different expiry dates. The portfolio manager would try to avoid having large options positions expire on the same day; however, an option trader would know from its price whether or not an option is likely to be exercised.

Traders of option portfolios are, among other things, trading volatility—their exposure is a function of how much interest rates, share prices or exchange rates are likely to move. Statistical pricing models for options will provide an 'implied' volatility which traders must measure against the actual volatility in the market, evident in the prevailing levels of premium.

RISKS

For an option seller, there is no credit risk outstanding once the buyer has paid the premium, although there is a very large market risk arising from the possibility that the buyer might exercise the option. Buyers bear the risk that sellers will not be able to fulfil their obligations under the contract when the time comes, ie, when the option is exercised. However, the seller has no control over whether or not the option is exercised.

PRACTICAL USE OF AN OPTION: SPECULATION

A speculator, anticipating a fall in futures prices, could buy a put option which means he or she has a short (sold) position, at the option strike price. For example, in April a speculator believes that interest rates have bottomed, so that interest-rate futures have peaked in price, but has reservations about selling futures contracts outright because that would bring an exposure to unlimited loss if prices rose further. Instead of selling futures, the speculator could buy ten June put options on 90-day bank bill futures, for a premium of, say, $250 per contract at a strike price of 93.00. If the options were in the money on the expiry date, ie, the price of June bank-bill futures was below the strike price of 93.00, the speculator would be assigned ten sold 90-day bank bill futures contracts at 93.00 (NB: only in-the-money options are exercised, out-of-the money and at-the-money options are left to expire worthless). To realise the profit, the speculator would then close the position by buying ten June futures contracts to close the position. The following would result:

Options bought in April, ten puts June strike 93.00 (yield 7%) premium cost 10 x $250 = $2500
Exercised in June on the date of the option expiry
Speculator is automatically assigned ten sold June futures contracts at the price of 93.00 (yield 7%): value $4915 162.99
Speculator buys ten June futures at 91.50 (yield 8.5%) to close the position
Value: $4 897 356.77
Profit: $17 806.17
Less outlay of $2500 (cost of premiums)
Net profit $15 306.17

Sophisticated option plays can be devised by combining such put and call options, exercisable at defined strike levels, eg, butterfly spread, bull spread, straddle (see 'Learning the Language').

PRACTICAL USE OF AN OPTION: HEDGING

A fund manager intending to buy bonds (at tender) in a couple of months runs a risk that bond prices might rise as market interest rates fall. To protect against this, the manager could set the purchase price now by buying call options on bond futures. The manager will be required to pay a premium for the options, which provide a hedge against a rise in the price of bonds. However, if bond prices fall, because interest rates have risen, the manager could abandon the call options and buy bonds at the lower price. The call option essentially puts a floor under the investment rate the manager will receive.

A borrower could also use options to hedge against rising interest rates which would cause bank-bill or fixed-interest securities to fall in price. A borrower would buy put options which put a cap on the borrower's interest cost. Again the option can be abandoned if lower market interest rates render the hedge unnecessary.

CHAPTER 6
EQUITY DERIVATIVES

Equity derivatives were introduced in Australia in 1976, with the launch of options over shares on the Australian Options Market, now ASX Derivatives, a division of the Australian Stock Exchange (ASX). Initially call options were listed over four stocks—BHP, Western Mining, CSR and Woodside Petroleum—then others were progressively added in line with investor demand. Put options were introduced in 1982. The list expanded to the point that in late 1994 ASX Derivatives offered put and call options over shares in 48 companies and three indexes. A new equity derivative arrived in Australia in 1983 when the Sydney Futures Exchange launched a share-price index (SPI) futures contract based on the barometer of the Australian sharemarket, ASX's All-Ordinaries index. Options on the SFE's SPI contract followed in 1985. The pace of development in equity derivatives quickened considerably in 1994 with the SFE and ASX Derivatives neck-and-neck in a race to secure the high ground in a growing market.

In May 1994 the SFE launched Individual Share Futures (ISFs), initially over three stocks, BHP, National Australia Bank and News Corporation, with a further four added a few months later: BTR Nylex, MIM Holdings, Westpac Banking Corporation and Western Mining. ASX Derivatives then announced the launch of a new product, a Low Exercise Price Option (LEPO) which while billed as a security carries the risk characteristics of a futures contract. The SFE challenged ASX Derivatives' capacity to trade such a product, taking the matter to court in

September 1994; in March 1995 the courts ruled in ASXD's favour and LEPOs could begin trading.

Meanwhile, ASX Derivatives, keen to push its role as the 'home of equity derivatives in Australia' in August 1994 announced its intention to launch Share Ratios, a new concept enabling investors to trade a specific stock's performance relative to the rest of the market, and so reduce market risk. Introduction of trading in Share Ratios was subject to regulatory approval which was granted early in 1995.

In addition to exchange-traded equity derivatives, a number of banks in Australia have begun offering over-the-counter equity swaps and options. By the end of 1994 investors in equities could choose from a range of derivatives to hedge or maximise their positions: over-the-counter products; at the SFE futures and options over the All-Ordinaries index and futures over individual shares (see chapter 2); and ASXD options over listed shares, long-term options, flex options, warrants and, in 1995, Share Ratios and LEPOs.

EXCHANGE-TRADED EQUITY OPTIONS

Equity options or options over listed shares offer a right, but not an obligation, to buy or sell a given parcel of shares at a set price (the strike or exercise price) at a predetermined date. As with other options, an equity option can be an option to buy (a call) or to sell (a put); thus a call option gives the right, but not the obligation, to buy a stipulated number of shares at a specified price on or before a set date; a put option gives the right, but not the obligation, to sell a stipulated number of shares at a specified price on or before a set date. The strike or exercise price of the option is the price at which the shares over which the option was written can be bought or sold, should the option holder decide to exercise.

The buyer (also known as taker) of an option pays a premium to the seller (writer or grantor) of the option. The premium represents the full extent of the buyer's potential loss. As with other options, equity options offer the chance for leverage, ie, taking a position in equities which is far larger than the initial outlay (the premium). The limited loss associated with buying (taking) options makes them very attractive to retail investors. Option sellers face potentially unlimited loss but they can modify their exposure by hedging/offsetting their risks in the market. Option sellers who have written call options carry the potential obligation to deliver (sell) shares to the option buyer because, should the buyer decide to exercise his or her right to buy the shares over which the option was written, the seller has to deliver these shares. In the case of a put option that is exercised, the seller of the option has to buy the stock from the option holder. Reflecting their greater exposure, sellers of options are usually required to lodge security, through their clearing member, with the Options Clearing House. Investors buying and selling options on the ASXD options market deal through ASX member organisations which have been approved as clearing members under ASX business rules to enter into option contracts on behalf of clients.

Options are identified by type, eg, put or call, by the name of the underlying shares, expiry date of the options and their strike price, eg, BHP October 1900 calls selling for 90 cents. Option prices are quoted in price per share, eg, if Company A calls trade at 50 cents, the value of an option contract (generally over 1000 shares) would be $500. Compare buying a parcel of shares with buying options over shares. To buy, say, 1000 Company A shares, assuming Company A is trading at $20 a share, a buyer would have to outlay $20 000 (1000 x Company A's share price of $20). But taking an option to buy or sell 1000 Company A shares would involve a fraction of that cost while still bringing the option holder control over 1000 shares. An illustration:

- BHP shares are at $20.00. The options have a June 1995 expiry and interest rates are assumed to be at 8 per cent and volatility at 20 per cent. The strike price is $20. Based on one of the option-pricing models, BHP call options would be $1.53 and puts 96 cents, so buying calls would cost $1 530 and buying puts $960, outlays which would provide control over 1000 BHP $20 shares.

The cost to the option buyer is the premium, which represents the intrinsic value and time value of the option, intrinsic value being the difference between the market value of the underlying shares and the expiry price of option. Come expiry date of the option, the buyer can choose to exercise the option or allow it to lapse. There is no obligation to exercise. Whether a buyer chooses to exercise or not would depend on whether the option were *in-the-money*, *at-the-money* or *out-of-the money*. (See chapter 5, option terminology.) For example, there would be no point in exercising a call option whose exercise price is above the prevailing market price for the underlying shares because the shares could be bought more cheaply on the market. The options would be left to lapse. Similarly, there is mileage in exercising put options only if their exercise price is above the market price for shares, enabling the option holder to sell at a higher-than-market price.

As discussed in chapter 5, several factors influence the value of an option. In the case of an equity option these are:

- the share price;
- the time to expiry of the option;
- the option's exercise price;
- dividends that might be paid before the option expires;
- likely level of interest rates during the option's life;
- volatility of the share price during the option's life (refer chapter 5 for details regarding pricing an option).

An option buyer is in a secure position compared with an option seller. It is the option holder's decision whether to exercise or not and if he or she decides to exercise his or her option to, say, buy the shares over which the option was written then the seller has to find the shares. If the option holder has an option to sell, and decides to exercise, then the option seller has to buy those shares to be sold according to the contract. An option seller (grantor or writer) has far greater exposure than an option buyer and would normally take steps to hedge his or her position. Because of this option sellers are for the most part, though not exclusively, major institutions whose sold (short) options form part of an options portfolio that is managed and monitored daily.

OPTIONS CLEARING HOUSE

The *Options Clearing House* (OCH) clears and registers contracts for ASX Derivatives, handles margining and risk management, and provides services whereby traders and investors can lodge collateral (securities, bank guarantees or financial instruments) as cover against their positions.

OCH uses TIMS (Theoretical Intermarket Margining System), developed in 1986 by Options Clearing Corporation, Chicago, as the first risk-based margining system to be applied to exchange-traded options. TIMS breaks margins into two components:

- *premium margin*, being the amount needed on any day to liquidate positions held, calculated using closing market prices; and
- *risk margin*, the additional margin required to cover a predetermined one-day market move in the underlying security.

Writers of options must lodge an initial deposit of at least $2000 with their clearing member; this is in addition to the margins levied by OCH on their positions. An option writer on ASX Derivatives can use collateral, eg, share scrip, to cover open positions, or lodge a bank guarantee of a minimum of $25 000 to cover margins or pledge fixed-interest securities through Austraclear Limited.

OCH calculates interest daily and pays interest on margins monthly with the interest rate based on prevailing market rates.

TYPES OF OPTIONS AVAILABLE ON ASX DERIVATIVES

Spot options

ASXD listed one-month 'spot' options in July 1991 over thirteen of its twenty-nine option stocks. These shorter contracts offer protection over limited periods in return for a modest outlay. They are useful as a way of taking cover, say, around the time a company is making an important announcement or some other factor is causing a stock price to fluctuate. Activity in spot options has been increasing and in 1994 represented about 10 per cent of turnover on the ASXD options market.

Long-term exchange-traded options

Long-term exchange-traded options (LTOs), listed on ASXD since October 1991, are available as two-year and three-year options over six stocks. LTOs have American-style exercise, are available as puts and calls and represent the standard 1000 shares a contract. Their exercise price is fairly close to the price of the underlying share at the time of listing and expiry coincides with the standard expiry month for options over the shares in question. LTOs are actively traded and in late 1994 accounted for 1.5 per cent of the turnover in options over the stocks in question. In June 1994 open positions in LTOs represented 5 per cent of turnover in options.

Index options

The first index options, on the Twenty Leaders index, were introduced in September 1992, with European-style exercise, cash-settlement and a $10 multiplier. Other index options followed, including the *Gold index* and *All-Ordinaries index*. Index options offer exposure to a broad market, rather than to a specific stock.

Flexible exchange-traded options

Introduced in January 1994, 'flex' options have varying characteristics determined by parties to the contract, such as variations in the underlying security, the exercise price, expiry date, exercise style (American or European), number of contracts and whether the options are puts or calls.

Warrants

Trading in warrants is facilitated by ASXD, which provides a marketplace through SEATS (Stock Exchange Automated Trading System), but the warrants are issued by a third party which is responsible for settlement when a warrant is exercised.

Warrants, hugely popular overseas, were introduced on the

ASX in 1990. The first issue, made in January 1991 by Macquarie
Bank Ltd, was a series of 15 million call warrants over shares
in Boral Ltd. Later that year Macquarie Bank made a second
issue, for 10 million call warrants over BHP shares. Bankers
Trust Australia Ltd issued the first index warrant to be traded
on the ASX when it launched four million call warrants over the
All-Ordinaries index in 1991. Equity warrants have proved the
most popular of the warrants written in Australia.

A warrant is similar to a long-dated option and generally has
a life somewhere between eighteen months and five years,
although there is no fixed time limit. Warrants work like options
issued by a third party which earns premium income for its role
and has to meet the obligations of settlement. The credit-standing of the issuer is vital, so the ASX has prescribed a list of
acceptable warrant issuers, which are restricted to banks
licensed by the Reserve Bank of Australia, governments or institutions with a guarantor which is a bank or government. Issuers
of warrants can choose whether or not to cover their exposure.
Warrants can be written over shares, share-price indexes, currencies or commodities. The crucial characteristic of a warrant
is that the issuer can show that the instrument would be defined
as a security under the Corporations Law. Like options, warrants
provide investors with a geared exposure to a share, share-price
index, currency or commodity in return for a limited outlay.
Because they are long-dated, warrants tend to carry a more
expensive premium than options. Warrants are settled either by
delivery of the underlying security or by cash payment; structure is at the discretion of the issuer. Exercise can be
European-style (exercisable only on expiry date), or American-
style, which enables the holder of the warrant to exercise at any
time before expiry date.

Warrants carry a similar risk profile to an option. With a call,
if the market price of the underlying security does not rise above
the exercise price of the warrant, plus premium and commission,
the holder gains nothing by exercising and the warrant expires
worthless. The same applies with a put where the market price
of the underlying has not fallen below the warrant's exercise
price.

SHARE RATIOS

Announced in August 1994 by ASX Derivatives, Share Ratios are tipped to create a new market in equities. They enable an investor to separate the specific risk associated with a particular stock from general market risk—to take a punt on which shares will outperform the market.

Share Ratio contracts, which ASXD claims as a world first, measure the performance of a given share against the All-Ordinaries index. They enable investors to trade relative share performance, which has become a popular way to measure investment returns. Market risk can be isolated, which is attractive to fund managers and hedgers as well as private investors. Using Share Ratio contracts, investors can gain exposure to a share's performance relative to the All-Ordinaries index, not to its rises and falls in price. Trading in Share Ratios was scheduled to begin with eight shares: ANZ Banking Group, BHP, CRA, National Australia Bank, MIM, News Corporation, Western Mining Corporation and Westpac Banking Corporation.

Changes in the Share Ratio price reflect the performance of the share in question to the overall market. An increase in the ratio price says that the share has performed better than the market, a decrease says it has underperformed compared to the market.

The Share Ratio formula:

$$\text{calculated ratio} = \frac{\text{share price cents}}{\text{All-Ordinaries index}} \times 1000$$

Example: National Australia Bank

NAB share price = $11.60, All-Ordinaries = 2010

$$\text{NAB ratio} = \frac{\text{NAB share price in cents}}{\text{All-Ordinaries}} \times 1000$$

$$= \frac{1160}{2010} \times 1000$$

$$= 577.1$$

Face value of a Share Ratio contract = market price* × $10

Example: NAB Share Ratio market price* = 578

NAB Share Ratio contract value = 578 × $10

= $5780

* The Share Ratio market price may trade at a discount or premium to the calculated ratio.

ASX Derivatives has described several benefits attached to Share Ratio contracts, including the reduction of exposure to overall market risk and the opportunity to hedge specific company risk during periods of potentially high volatility such as the company reporting season or when the government is announcing sensitive economic data. A portfolio can be adjusted using Share Ratios instead of physically selling shares and realising profits or losses, which can be useful for tax purposes. Share Ratios can be arbitraged against shares, options and futures and short-term switches of shares can be undertaken without unwinding existing positions.

The introduction of Share Ratios was facilitated by advances in ASX systems which enable Share Ratios to be traded through the exchange's SEATS and cleared and margined through the Options Clearing House using TIMS. Buyers and sellers of Share Ratios are exposed to potential profits and losses so they have to lodge with the OCH an initial margin of about 5 per cent of the face value of the ratio contract, depending on the Share Ratio traded. Variation margins are calculated daily and posted to the clearing member's account like a mark-to-market position (a credit if the market has moved in the trader's favour, a debit if against). Cash or collateral such as share scrip, bank bills or other acceptable securities can be lodged with the Options Clearing House to cover the initial margin, whereas the subsequent margin requirements of Share Ratio contracts (mark-to-market postings) must be covered by cash.

LEPOS

A Low Exercise Price Option (LEPO) is in the form of a call (buy) option with a very low strike (exercise) price, usually between one and ten cents, and is exercisable only on the last day of trading before expiry. LEPOs are deliverable, not cash-settled. A LEPO is in the form of an option in the sense that a buyer pays a premium at the outset and retains the right to exercise or not. And, like an option or a futures contract, a LEPO offers control of a parcel of shares (1000 per LEPO contract) for considerably less than the face value of the parcel. In its risk profile, though, a LEPO is more like a futures contract than an option. A characteristic of a LEPO is its low exercise price, consequently high premium (see example below) and very high leverage. However, while the premium may be high, the investor does not pay the full amount of the premium but only a margin which is adjusted on a mark-to-market basis as the LEPO changes price. The buyer of a LEPO is margined (pays a risk margin) daily according to ASX Derivatives' mark-to-market system (TIMS).

Day 1: An investor buys a LEPO over BHP shares which are trading at $17. The strike price is 10 cents so the premium would be $16.90 (excluding time value for the sake of simplicity) so a buyer would outlay $16.90 × 1000 or $16 900. The buyer's account with his or her broker is debited for the premium of $16 900—but the investor is reimbursed for most of that amount at the end of the first day, as follows:

At the end of day one BHP's share price has fallen to $16.85 so under the mark-to-market process the LEPO is revalued and the investor's account credited with $16 850. The investor has a loss of $50 (had the price risen, the investor would have been credited the appropriate amount). The investor is charged an additional margin to cover potential future paper losses—$400, a sum calculated by OCH using TIMS and drawing on various inputs including historical volatility and market sentiment—so for effectively $400 the investor is controlling a parcel of 1000 BHP shares which is the same risk profile as if he or she had taken out a futures contract. Day one ends with the investor having outlaid an initial margin of $400.

Day two: BHP shares are down to $16.70 so effectively the investor is showing a 20-cent loss × 1000 which is $200 so OCH debits his or her account $200. That must be paid to OCH. At this stage the investor has a contract worth $16.70 a share (market price), has outlaid a deposit of $400 and incurred a loss of $200.

Day three: BHP drops to $16.40 a share, a loss of 30 cents a share or $300 on contract value.

Day four: BHP rallies and the price rises to $16.95, an increase of 55 cents or $550 (× 1000 shares) which is credited to the investor's account. The $400 initial margin (good faith money) is set aside. At this stage the investor is $50 in front (losses totalled $500 and gains $550). Had the price continued to fall the investor would have continued to lose and it is against this possibility that the Options Clearing House holds the $400 which is deemed sufficient to cover a one-day move in the share price. The BHP share price would have to fall by 40 cents to create a $400 debit. Using TIMS, OCH assesses the likely one-day fall in a share price and charges the initial margin accordingly. The $400 initial deposit is similar to the initial margin on a futures contract and, as with futures, it varies with market volatility.

Professional investors (large companies and institutions whose business includes buying and selling shares and other investments) can benefit from the OCH's margining system, which takes into account any offsetting positions. For example, a professional investor might buy a LEPO and be asked for a $400 initial deposit as in the above example but because he or she is holding other positions in BHP shares—say, has granted (sold) call options—OCH takes the overall risk exposure into account. The investor has a LEPO with a very high delta but has sold three exchange-traded options with a lower delta (bearing in mind that delta is the amount by which an option increases or decreases in value relative to a small change in the value of the underlying share) so the overall position is 0.99 long (LEPO) and 0.9 (3 × 0.3) short so the difference is 0.09 × 400 = net exposure. However, OCH would look at the investor's whole option portfolio and assess what cover is needed. A retail trader would be unlikely to be granting call options so has not the same potential to offset positions.

Offset is allowed between the following in the same underlying security:

- written (granted) and taken (bought) call options;
- written and taken put options;
- written calls and taken put options; and
- written puts and taken call options.

OVER-THE-COUNTER EQUITY DERIVATIVES

Over-the-counter (OTC) equity derivatives are typically used by managers of equity portfolios, fund managers, institutional investors and companies exposed to the sharemarket through strategic holdings in other companies as well as individuals with sizeable equity holdings. Generally OTC equity derivatives are provided by financial institutions which specialise in structuring equity products and in market-making and are skilled in managing their own equity-related risk.

Equity swaps

In 1989 Bankers Trust introduced the concept of an equity swap and since then variations of this basic structure have emerged. Equity swaps, common in the US and Europe, are not as widely used as interest-rate, currency or commodity swaps in the Australian market. However, their use is increasing, particularly by institutions looking for an alternative to trading SPI futures. An equity swap shares the characteristics of other swaps: notional principal, specified term, predetermined payments made at intervals, a fixed rate (swap coupon) and a floating rate based on an acknowledged index—in the case of equity swaps a share index such as S&P 500, Nikkei, London FT Index or in Australia the All-Ordinaries index, or to a sub-index such as the All Industrials. As with other swaps, an equity swap involves the exchange of two income streams.

A basic equity swap would involve an end-user and an equity swaps dealer. The end-user, Aussie Management Co, has a diversified share portfolio whose return is much in line with the All-Ordinaries index but Aussie Management Co wants to receive a fixed rate of return. Aussie Management Co can enter into a swap with a dealer, agreeing to pay the All-Ordinaries-related return and receive a fixed rate of return for the term of the swap. Payments will be made quarterly on the notional principal which stays the same for the life of the swap. The notional principle is not exchanged and is used merely as a base to calculate the regular payments.

Using an equity-for-fixed-equity swap, Aussie Management Co has converted the unpredictable return from its share portfolio into a stable fixed-interest return. Under the swap agreement, if the return on equities is negative in a quarter, the swap dealer pays Aussie Management Co the percentage change in the value of the notional principal (index) and the swap coupon on the fixed leg of the deal. A variation of the above is the equity-for-floating-equity swap, which is similarly structured except that instead of a fixed leg there is a leg tied to a floating-rate index such as BBSW or LIBOR. As is the practice of dealers in other types of swaps, equity swap dealers hedge their risk, in their case by trading SPI futures.

Equity options

OTC equity options are structured in the same way as other options with the buyer paying a premium to the seller in return for the right to buy or sell a specific parcel of shares, or a basket of shares, or an index, at a specified price on or before a set date. (In the case of an option over an index, the option would be cash-settled.) As with all OTC products, OTC equity options can be tailored to suit individual investors' preferences, providing, for example, a specific maturity date and notional principal and the flexibility to be written over a variety of assets (basket of stocks, index and so on). Banks offer OTC equity options to clients keen to protect the price risk of equity portfolios such as institutional equity managers, fund managers and, increasingly, Australian corporate clients. These option buyers might buy a put and offset the cost of the premium by selling a call (a collar), or buy a put spread. The variations continue. Also, there is a growing range of structured products such as equity-index-linked notes (eg, ASPRIN, see 'Learning the Language') and bonds whose return is linked to some other type of equity asset.

Equity derivatives traded on the Sydney Futures Exchange are discussed in chapter 2.

CHAPTER 7

DERIVATIVES AND COMMODITIES

Banks' increasing interest in commodity markets as a source of demand for derivative products partly reflects the changing role of a number of commodity marketing boards; as these boards cease to protect producers from fluctuation in commodity prices, banks are seeking to offer commodity producers derivatives products to manage price risks.

Reserve Bank of Australia study 'Australian banks activities in derivatives markets: products and risk-management practices'.

Derivatives, which have recently become closely identified with the financial markets, have been used in commodity markets, in the form of forwards and options, for hundreds of years. Grain futures began trading on a formalised exchange in the US when the Chicago Board of Trade opened in 1848. Cotton futures followed in 1870, coffee in 1882 and sugar in 1914. The London Metals Exchange (LME) opened for business in 1877.

Commodity derivatives began trading in Australia when the Sydney Greasy Wool Futures Exchange, now the Sydney Futures Exchange, opened in 1960 to trade wool futures contracts. Wool futures trading, sidelined by the reserve price scheme which prevailed from 1972 to 1991, has been revitalised on the Sydney Futures Exchange with a new deliverable contract. The SFE's trading link with the giant New York Mercantile Exchange brings Nymex's extremely active oil contract, based on West Texas Intermediate, into the Asia–Pacific region for the first time. In 1994 Nymex merged with New York's Commodity Exchange (Comex), the major gold and silver exchange, in a move that took the merged entity to the position of dominant commodities exchange and fifth-largest futures exchange in the world. Gold and silver appear as natural additions to the SFE's list of contracts. That development, combined with the trend of increasing focus on base metals in the market and by SFE members, suggests that the SFE's commodity complex could well build on wool and oil and extend to base metals and, in due course, coal. The two exchanges plan to build on common goals: the SFE is keen to position itself as the premier commodity exchange in the Asia–Pacific region, while for Nymex/Comex, having links in the growing Asia–Pacific region is strategically important.

Australia, as a major commodity exporter, has developed considerable expertise in derivatives applicable to commodities. And since most commodities are priced in $US, producers are exposed to, and have become used to coping with, exchange-rate as well as commodity-price risk. The Australian Wheat Board is active in the over-the-counter currency options market to hedge its export income as well as being a regular user of the big wheat futures markets in Chicago, Kansas and Minneapolis and of the French wheat swaps market. Gold producers have long used forward selling as a way of fixing future prices. Australian mining companies have used the London Metals Exchange for some twenty years. The cotton-marketing groups offer forward prices to growers and the marketers hedge their exposures.

Whereas the increasing use of derivatives in financial markets has prompted concerns among regulators and central bankers that these instruments could exacerbate instability, in commodity markets derivatives have long been regarded as essential for efficiency. Commodity markets operators are inured to volatility; they operate confidently in an area that is vulnerable to fluctuations in supply and demand and to influences outside human control, such as the weather. Anything that can be used to reduce risk and uncertainties is welcomed.

Commodities can be divided into hard and soft and energy products. Hard commodities are precious metals, such as gold and silver, and base metals including aluminium, copper, zinc, tin, nickel and lead. Soft commodities include wool and grains such as wheat, sugar and corn. Many commodity producers and consumers tend to avoid the more exotic derivative concoctions that crop up increasingly in financial markets, taking the view that the more exotic structures involve a view of where the market is heading and so are more akin to a bet. On the other side, a 1994 Reserve Bank survey of Australian banks' activities in derivatives showed only minor, although growing, activity in derivatives written against underlying markets other than exchange rates and interest rates. 'Derivatives written against precious metals, base metals, equities and other commodities make up just 2 per cent of aggregate activity. Only eight of the 38 banks in the survey reported any involvement in these markets', the RBA commented. But it added:

> Banks' increasing interest in commodity markets as a source of demand for derivative products partly reflects the changing role of a number of commodity marketing boards; as these boards cease to protect producers from fluctuation in commodity prices, banks are seeking to offer commodity producers derivatives products to manage price risks.

Producers generally make prudent use of derivatives. Conscious that hedging financial risk is not their core business, most of the mining houses stick to fairly straightforward techniques— although there is always an exception to the rule—such as forwards and options. They are looking to protect a physical risk and to diminish a business risk, not create additional risk. Producers hedge to create greater certainty in returns and protect margins so that shareholders benefit. Their bottom line is risk management, so transactions are structured off a physical position.

The gold-mining community is often cited as one that is highly sophisticated and makes good use of hedging opportunities. Many of the largest operators have quite conservative boards which are unfamiliar with all but the most basic products and that constrains their use of derivatives. The treasury division might understand derivatives but can be discouraged if the board is not comfortable with them. Some companies have had bad experiences in hedging and have become wary of the process. However, the overall benefit of hedging has been not only positive but instrumental in the rapid growth of the modern Australian gold-mining industry. Even so, companies have to be aware that shareholders are likely to criticise hedging when the market is rising, then become nervous when the gold price is falling. Bearing in mind that gold is denominated in $US, companies have to consider whether their shareholders want to be exposed to the $A or $US price of gold. Companies can hedge their foreign-exchange exposure, leaving shareholders exposed only to fluctuations in the gold price.

Some producers are happy to maintain a passive hedging policy, rather than aggressively trying to pick highs and lows. Others—a small percentage—do not hedge at all, but wear fluctuations in the gold price in the belief that that is what their shareholders want. This approach is now the exception, whereas in the early 1980s a company that consistently hedged was the odd one out. Any producer considering using the more exotic derivatives should first have in place the systems to be able to manage and monitor these; such an active approach smacks more of dealing, which raises the question of whether a corporate's treasury division should try to be as active, in terms of equipment and approach, as that of a bank. Generally, it is accepted that, unlike banks, companies do not operate a treasury as a profit centre, instead directing it towards risk management.

Investor perception is important for a gold-mining company. If shareholders and analysts perceive a company as one that hedges, and the company suddenly changes policy and does not hedge, the company risks losing support. Conversely, a company that is known as one that eschews hedging will risk upsetting shareholders if it springs on a hedging policy just as the gold price rises. Some investors expect mining companies to do well or badly in line with the trend in commodity prices. Some companies say they are criticised for putting in place a hedging policy that prevents shareholders from participating in a price rise, but at the same time win no praise for undertaking hedging to minimise a downturn—even though that is the prudent course of action. It is a question of expectations. A solution, it has been suggested, is for companies to leave hedging up to individual investors.

Smaller gold-mining companies have less flexibility than larger mining houses whose diversification of interests is in itself something of a hedge. For a major mining house, a fall in the gold price could be offset by a rise in the price of aluminium or copper, so it might hedge less than its smaller counterparts.

But a small gold-mining company, perhaps with only one mine, is highly exposed to that mine and the revenues it produces and it is very likely that a lending bank would require such a company to take out some element of hedging to protect its revenue, leaving it exposed only to production risk. Also, many Australian mines have a limited life so there are only so many years during which the investment can be paid back.

Most corporates try to find a balance between spending on the latest technology to equip a sophisticated dealing room and simply having a well-trained treasury staff able to understand the products offered by their banks. Commodity producers say they prefer to use products which can be explained to a board and chief executive in a few plain-English sentences. For mining companies, treasury's chief task is to ensure funds are available to meet the daily liquidity needs of the company and its longer-term projects. Essential for any company is deciding on a hedging policy to follow, spelling out the rationale for hedging, having the necessary controls in place and procedures for checking that these are effective. Gold-mining companies which have facilities with banks which are margined (ie, a margin call is made by the bank if the mark-to-market value of the company's contracts moves out of the money by more than, say, $50–$100 an ounce) must understand the effect of the derivatives products they are using on these facilities. Many new derivatives products move out of the money more quickly than, say, a forward contract, so a company could find itself using up more credit more quickly. And companies should set limits and ensure these are adhered to. Companies are also encouraged to mark their derivative exposures to market, if only for internal purposes. They should be alert to the possibility of entering into a new derivative product before having the software needed to be able to mark it to market.

A recent trend has been an increasingly commercial focus on the part of government departments. This is reflected in their growing interest in hedging so that they can more accurately budget for energy costs, such as diesel fuel for buses and trains. Given that most fuel supplies are sourced in Australia they would be hedging interest-rate, rather than foreign-exchange, exposures.

HOW SWAPS AND OPTIONS ARE USED

Hedgers in commodities use over-the-counter (OTC) swaps, forwards and options, and futures contracts where they suit. Commodity markets in general lag interest-rate and foreign-exchange markets in the use of exotics. Broadly, though, whatever can be used in the interest-rate and currency swap market can probably be applied to the commodity markets, but the feature often lacking is the depth of the underlying market in which to hedge and rehedge. A bank carrying out an interest-rate swap can easily hedge in the market but there is less ability to do so in many commodities. However, the flexibility varies with the markets. For example, in oil, West Texas Intermediate crude and Brent are active benchmark crudes, with WTI traded on the New York Mercantile Exchange (Nymex), the largest energy futures exchange in the world, and Brent on the International Petroleum Exchange (IPE) in London. Both offer good liquidity. With Tapis, the Malaysian benchmark light crude, there is no futures exchange facilitating the purchase or sale of futures against the product—hedging in Tapis has been likened to the $A swaps market of the early 1980s when a bank made a fixed price and could only offset its risk by approaching another over-the-counter market-maker. The Singapore International Monetary Exchange (Simex) lists a high-sulphur fuel futures contract but it trades only a few hundred contracts a day. The Asia–Pacific region will be able to trade the world benchmark crude oil price in its own timezone when the proposed trading link between the SFE and Nymex gets under way in 1995, enabling SFE members to trade Nymex's highly liquid WTI futures contract.

COMMODITY SWAPS

Commodity swaps are still in a growth phase compared with the volume transacted in interest-rate and currency markets, where swaps have become a mature product. To commodity producers, a swap is a long-range forward sale: a commodity price is fixed against a benchmark price or index for the commodity. Others liken a commodity swap to a single interest-rate swap—the two parties agree on a fixed price and cash-settlement against a floating index. In the case of an oil swap, parties agree a fixed monthly price for, say, WTI, and every month one would receive (the other pay) a cash settlement based on the difference between that fixed price and the daily average WTI quoted on Nymex. Under the swap agreement counterparty A makes periodic payments to counterparty B at a fixed price per unit of a specified commodity for a notional amount of that commodity. Counterparty B pays A a floating price per unit for a notional amount of that commodity, which is generally an average price derived from the recent trend in the spot price. The counterparties do not exchange the commodities (which are usually the same but could be different); all exchanges take place in cash. In practice, A and B are unlikely to be known to each other, with the transaction arranged and managed by an intermediary (see figure 7.1).

The method for cash-settlement of a commodity swap differs from that applied to financial instruments. For example, whereas an interest-rate swap might settle against the three-month LIBOR rate every three months, many commodity markets use an averaging process daily or weekly so that the hedge more closely replicates the risks the hedging company is running. This reflects the greater volatility in commodity markets compared with even interest-rate and currency markets. Base metals and energy markets experience a volatility of between 15 and 35 per cent compared with about 8 to 12 per cent in interest rates and currencies.

Example

Counterparty A is a crude oil producer which wants to fix the price it receives for its production for three years. Each month A produces, on average, 5000 barrels of oil. Meanwhile, Counterparty B, an oil refiner, wants to fix the price it will pay for oil for three years. B needs some 8000 barrels of oil a month. The two enter into a swap with an intermediary (swaps dealer); this has no effect on their normal activities in the physical oil market. When the two initiate their swap the intermediary's mid-price for the relevant oil is $18.25 a barrel. B agrees to make

Figure 7.1 Example of an oil swap and oil market transactions

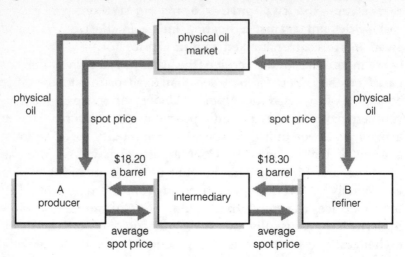

monthly payments to the intermediary at $18.30 a barrel and the intermediary agrees to pay B an amount equal to the average daily spot price for oil over the preceding month. At the same time, A agrees to pay the intermediary an amount equal to the average daily spot price for oil over the preceding month in exchange for payments from the intermediary at the rate of $18.20 a barrel. Effectively these payments fixed the price of the oil for both A and B. The intermediary offsets its own risk by entering into a third swap as a fixed-price payer on 3000 barrels of oil (the difference in quantity between the two swaps). Or, in the absence of a suitable counterpary, the intermediary can hedge using oil futures.

COMMODITY OPTIONS

Options can be bought and sold over commodities as they can over financial instruments. A typical option for a commodity consumer would be to agree to a fixed-rate $US strike for, say, aluminium (base metals and bullion are quoted in $US) which cash-settles once a month against a daily average of the London Metals Exchange spot price. With metals, hedges are available out to two or three years, although most hedging would be between one and two years. Short-term options are more common in energy markets and apart from those hedging against WTI and Brent, liquid hedges are available only out to twelve months.

Options in commodities are available in the usual range of caps, floors and collars. A consumer would typically buy a commodity cap to set a maximum price to be paid, whereas producers buy floors because they want to set a minimum future price for production and sales. The more sophisticated structures, such as look-back, barrier and average options are also available (see 'Learning the Language').

HARD COMMODITIES

Gold

Gold is treated as a currency—in certain countries in the Middle East and Asia it *is* a currency—and whatever derivatives can be applied to currency and financial instruments can be applied to gold.

Australia is the third-largest gold producer in the world, after South Africa and the US, and ranks in output with the Commonwealth of Independent States (CIS, the former Soviet Union). Most producers hedge against price fluctuations. Gold producers in Australia sell their gold to banks (intermediaries such as Republic Mase, Macquarie Bank, Rothschild Australia Ltd) in the form of 995 account metal (which is much like a paper transfer of money). The banks then request a refinery, such as Johnson Matthey, the Perth Mint or Golden West, to manufacture the gold into a bar; gold bars are available in a variety of types including good delivery bar (one that meets the requirements of the London Bullion Market Association), kilo bar (a 1-kilogram bar of gold, good for jewellery), ten-tola bar (3.75 ounces, an Indian denomination used widely in the Asian markets) and large bars. Banks mostly request kilo bars. Much of the gold is shipped to Asia for jewellery and manufacturing. Asian nations traditionally buy and horde gold and a large proportion of Australian production is absorbed into that region. Or the bank might receive loco Australian gold (gold priced for delivery in Australia) which it can ship to Singapore in exchange for loco London gold (gold priced for delivery in London). Diagrammatically:

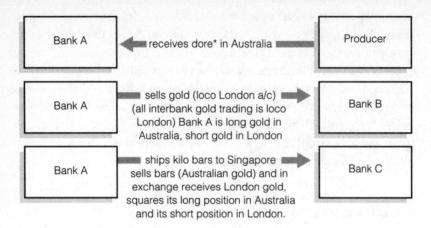

Bank A	◄ receives dore* in Australia ◄	Producer
Bank A	sells gold (loco London a/c) ► (all interbank gold trading is loco London) Bank A is long gold in Australia, short gold in London	Bank B
Bank A	ships kilo bars to Singapore ► sells bars (Australian gold) and in exchange receives London gold, squares its long position in Australia and its short position in London.	Bank C

* the impure alloy of gold and silver which is refined to pure gold

Gold is a 24-hour market—as Comex closes in New York the market opens in Australia, then in Japan, Hong Kong, Zurich and London, with Hong Kong trading every Saturday. From an interbank perspective, the market in Australia is at times considerably less liquid than, say, the foreign-exchange market and is certainly less liquid than the markets in Europe and the US. Although not seeing the volumes traded in these major markets, there is considerable demand for cover during the Australian day, reflecting the 24-hour nature of the gold market. Intermediaries in this country provide a market-making service after the major New York market closes (4.30am Australian winter time, 6.30am summer time) filling the time slot between the Comex close and the opening of the London markets. In this they are progressively joined by the Asian centres Tokyo, Hong Kong and Singapore. The market undergoes something of a 'twilight' after New York closes, with only the Australian market quoting until Tokyo opens and activity picks up after that with four major centres making markets. Most activity takes place in the first and last hours of trading on Comex.

Derivatives activity in gold in Australia is largely over-the-counter, privately negotiated between bullion bank and client, with Comex regarded as more of a market for traders and speculators than for producers. (Producers, particularly the smaller mining houses, are discouraged from using Comex by the prospect of having to meet margin calls on futures contracts.) A difference for intermediaries in the gold market in Australia is that whereas their New York counterparts have grown up around trading gold and dealing with the more speculative end of the market, Australian gold banks have grown around the mining industry. Since 1982 that growth has been spectacular: from 25 tonnes a year to 250 in 1994, providing fresh opportunities.

A fundamental factor behind the growth in the derivatives market in gold is the availability of a large stock of physical gold for borrowing in the form of central bank holdings of some 30 000 to 40 000 tonnes and private deposits. These stable holdings are large compared with worldwide annual production of around 2000 tonnes. The borrowing or lease market for gold is global and quite liquid, with rates typically around 1 per cent. Thus bullion banks can borrow metal, sell spot and generate cash to invest in the capital markets. In early 1995 Australian investment rates varied from about 7 per cent for cash to more than 10 per cent for long bonds, creating a substantial net difference between the cost of borrowing gold and the investment returns on funds. This net return comprises the gold contango (forward prices higher than prices for near months) which in turn determines the forward market in gold.

The Australian gold market is well developed in terms of its use of derivative products, with demand boosted by investor interest as well as end-user needs and by the derivative houses enthusiastically marketing hedging products and techniques. Banks and bullion houses intermediate between the central bank and the gold-mining houses which do not have direct access to the central bank. Gold producers have markedly lifted their use of hedging since the late 1980s with a consequent improvement in their business, reduction in their risk profile and increase in the number of mines being opened. Gold producers in Australia are often cited as an example of an industry that has taken a sensible and positive approach to derivatives, using them to hedge an underlying exposure by, say, buying puts and granting call options against gold they have in the ground.

Example: gold-mining company secures price protection by buying put options

Gold is trading spot at $400 and a gold-mining company buys European-style put options with a strike price of $390. If the gold price is below $390 when the option expires, the option holder can exercise and sell at $390, ie, at a better-than-market price. If the market holds above $390 the gold-mining company holding the options can sell at the market price and has lost only the cost of the premiums (say, $5 an ounce for a six-month option) paid for the protection provided by the option.

As with other options, the premium (cost) of a gold option is based on a combination of factors: the spot price of gold, the strike price, prevailing interest rates, time to expiry of the option and the expected volatility of the gold price (the unknown factor). Option dealers use a model such as the Black–Scholes pricing model to work out premiums. Gold options, like all options, offer an option buyer huge leverage: for a modest initial outlay—the premium paid to the option seller—a buyer can build up a significant position in gold.

Example: call option

Gold is trading at $400 spot and call options with a strike price of $425 can be bought for a premium of, say, $17.50 for a one-year option or $2.25 for a three-month option. If the spot price of gold rises to $425 during the life of the option then the option is at-the-money; if the price rises to $450 then the option is in-the-money and would be exercised because that enables the option holder to buy gold at $425 when the prevailing market price is $450; if the gold price fell to $400 then the option is out-of-the money, there is no value in exercising and the option would be allowed to lapse.

The above are very basic examples of put and call options. More complex strategies can be constructed using combinations of these. The more sophisticated the strategy, the more stringent must be the monitoring and controls over option positions to ensure that all bases are covered and no new and unforeseen exposures inadvertently created.

Hedging gold is part of the core business of gold producers, enabling them to plan and develop new projects without having to surrender equity. Typically, the gold producers hedge only a proportion of their reserves, usually around 60 or 70 per cent. Their strategy would take account of the gold price and its direction, the cost of production, the cost of borrowing gold and interest-rate exposure during the term of the forward or option used.

Gold banks offer producers a full range of derivatives from forwards, options, options combined with forwards, par or flat forwards, step forwards, spot-deferred facilities (rolling funding arrangements structured with no fixed term but which could stay in place for five years with the rate periodicially renegotiated) or whatever combination suits. A deferred facility usually has a maximum term equal to the mine-life of the producer, provided no breach of contract occurs in that time. Forward selling under this type of facility may have one or several interest-rate settings. Under deferred facilities gold can be sold forward for up to ten years. A par or flat forward, which evens out the price curve (income stream, which is normally in contango, ie, forward prices higher than prices for near months) to provide a constant price for the life of the transaction, is popular with gold producers: it provides not just steady cashflow but brings some income forward so that a producer can reduce borrowing costs by being able to repay debt earlier. A step forward is similar to a par or flat forward but instead of providing one constant price it provides several, so that forward cashflows are tailored more closely to a producer's requirements. With forwards, a gold bank buys gold for a forward delivery date from a gold producer.

Gold forward

A gold producer typically sells gold forward to its bank, fixing a price now for gold to be produced in, say, six months' time. Gold is usually in contango, ie, forward prices are higher than spot prices; the contango comprises two elements:

- the cash interest rate expressed in the currency in which gold is being sold forward. Assume the producer sells gold forward in $A for delivery in six months' time ($A six-month interest rate is 9.25 per cent);
- the cost of borrowing gold for six months, say, 0.80 per cent (80 points).

A gold producer selling gold forward to a bank creates several exposures which the bullion bank must manage. One way would be as follows:

- *spot price movement risk*: the forward price offered to the gold producer is built up from the spot price of gold when the forward is priced by the bank. So, because the forward price offered to the producer is fixed, any future movement in the spot gold price generates a profit or loss to the bank if the bank does not hedge this risk. Thus gold bought forward by a bank from a producer is sold into the spot gold market at or close to the time the forward is agreed. In this way the bank protects itself from any fall in the gold price while giving up any potential profit should the gold price rise.
- *cash interest rate and third-currency risk*: hedging the spot gold price as above results in the bank being short (has sold) gold and, because the interbank gold market is quoted in $US per ounce of gold, is long (has bought) $US. In this example the gold producer has sold gold forward in $A. So the bank sells the $US generated by the spot hedge of gold and buys $A which are invested for the period of the forward contract, attracting the 9.25 per cent six-month rate. The bank passes this interest rate on to the producer through the forward price quoted on the gold.
- *gold funding risk*: the bank has sold gold it will not receive for six months from the producer. To do this the bank borrows gold, at an interest rate determined by supply and demand. The charge to the bank for borrowing or sourcing the gold is also factored into the forward price offered to the producer. Assume the borrowing cost of gold is 0.80 per cent,

$$\$495 \times \left[\frac{9.25\% \times \frac{180}{365} + 1}{0.80\% \times \frac{180}{360*} + 1} - 1 \right] = \$20.518$$

*Gold and $US are traded on a 360-day year.

(The bank would also charge the producer a credit margin for the transaction which would reduce the contango. However, the credit margin varies from customer to customer so for simplicity it is omitted from this transaction.)

Added to the spot gold price of $495, this achieves a forward price in six months of $515.52 an ounce of gold for the gold sold forward by the producer. At the end of the six months the producer delivers the gold to the bank and receives $515.52 an ounce. The bank uses that gold to repay the borrowing it had earlier taken out and matures the $A investment to pay the producer for its gold.

Producers also use a range of option techniques to leverage forward prices or generate premium income. The forward book is managed, monitored and massaged daily. The gold borrowing cost is an important and variable component of forwards. The gold market is deep enough for a producer to be able to get cover for its metal borrowing cost as far forward as ten years; however, this is unlikely because the cost would be prohibitive. The metal borrowing market is very liquid out to two years but thin between two and five years and this is reflected in high costs. Most producers choose to fund their metal borrowing requirements for periods of less than twelve months, taking the view that costs do not justify funding for longer. For example, a three-month metal borrowing cost averaged 0.75 per cent per annum between 1990 and 1994 while the three-year rate averaged 1.4 per cent per annum. Most banks would fund a producer who chose to fix the metal borrowing cost for three years, believing they could achieve a funding cost below the rate charged to the producer.

Options used in the gold market are based on European puts and calls, transacted over-the-counter. Very few producers are active buyers of, say, New York Commodity Exchange (Comex) options, although they can buy these through an intermediary. Generally, producers prefer options that are tailored to their needs in terms of size, maturity date and strike price. Producers use combinations of puts, calls and forwards to achieve the desired outcomes. These combinations typically result in zero-cost structures which are attractive to gold producers, given that the metal is in contango. For example, a producer may protect against downside by buying a strip of put options (say, monthly over twelve months) and pay for the puts by granting a similar strip of call options at higher prices. The put strike is fixed, while the call strike will be determined according to the volume of calls the producer thinks it prudent to grant (noting that the producer gives away upside above the call strike price). The structure that results may involve something as simple as one put and one call, or involve various ratios of puts and calls (ratio options). If price-maximisation is an objective, the producer may enter into a strip of forwards (at contango) and grant additional call options whose premium is used to further increase the forward price. Such structures enable a producer to leverage his natural long gold position.

A common example of a ratio option is one where a producer buys one put option for every two call options granted (sold) to the bank. All options in this structure have the same strike price. Assume the $A spot gold price is $485, the forward price is $513 and the option maturity date September 1995:

Pricing

Put options premium (using Black–Scholes option-pricing model) is $18.30 an ounce, call options premium is $9.15 an ounce. Strike price for both is $520.

Option type	premium $	ounces	total premium $	strike price $
put	18.30	5 000	91 500.00	$520
call	9.15	10 000	91 500.00	$520
Total premium due			183 000.00	

Results on maturity

If the $A spot gold price is less than $520 the producer exercises the put option, sells 5000 ounces of gold at $520, ie above the prevailing market price. The call options expire worthless.

If the $A spot gold price is higher than $520 the put option expires worthless, the bank exercises its right to the call options (because it can buy them below market) so the producer sells 10 000 ounces of gold at $520 to the bank. In most instances the bank would enter a spot-deferred facility with the producer so that the producer is not locked into selling at a below-market price.

The ratio option provides the producer with a better price than would have been achieved had he written a forward contract at $513. Whatever the outcome, the producer is able to sell gold at $520, although he has to wear some exposure through granting the call options.

Gold loans

Initially provided in Australia by Mase Westpac (later Republic Mase), Macquarie Bank and Rothschild, these were widely used by mining companies in the early-to-mid-1980s as a way of raising capital. With a gold loan a mining company borrows gold from a bank (which can borrow the gold from the central bank), sells it spot, which produces immediate cash, and promises to deliver a portion of its future production to the bank to repay the bank loan and interest. Because gold could be borrowed at rates as low as 2 or 3 per cent, this was much cheaper than borrowing funds so the gold-miner was able to secure cheaper funding than if it borrowed cash (although that could change if the cost of borrowing gold rose). A gold loan is also a gold-price hedge for the volume borrowed and sold. In the 1990s gold loans tend to be used less frequently, mainly because most producers run hedge books comprising at least a proportion of forwards, so they may have adequate gold-price protection. The contango earned on the forwards offsets the extra cost of borrowing money rather than gold. Thus a cash loan backed by forward sales (a synthetic gold loan) generates the same outcome for a gold producer as a gold loan, and the combination of cash and gold forward may be more flexible.

Gold futures

Gold futures were introduced on the Sydney Futures Exchange in 1978, four years after a gold contract was introduced on the New York Commodity Exchange (Comex). Gold futures on the SFE rode the gold boom-and-bust that saw the price of the precious metal crack the $US500–an-ounce barrier in December 1979 and climb to more than $US800 in January 1980, only to crash later that month to $US470. The SFE enjoyed frenzied trading levels which were repeated in September 1980 when uncertainties in the Middle East sent the price back up to more than $US700. After 1981, though, the gold market turned quiet.

On the SFE, the share-price index futures contract, introduced in 1983, became the star performer, drawing considerable liquidity. In 1985 the SFE signed what was seen at the time as a milestone agreement, establishing a trading link with Comex to trade its highly liquid gold futures contract, used by speculators and traders from around the world. The move, though, did not live up to expectations, partly because the contract did not attract sufficient local liquidity, partly because the gold market was in a lull and partly because when the link was struck Comex's volumes were suffering from the fallout of a member failure and never recovered. In 1989 the link was suspended. The SFE's trading link with Nymex, which in 1994 merged with Comex, heralds the possibility of renewed vitality in gold futures in Sydney, based on the greater interaction between exchanges facilitated by electronic screen-dealing systems and buoyant gold prices in late 1994.

Silver

Every product offered in gold is also available in silver but the demand for hedging products over silver is considerably lower. Australia is not a large silver producer and moreover silver, priced at $5 an ounce compared with gold's $400+, is constantly under threat of losing its status as a precious metal. Silver is highly volatile and so attracts substantial speculative interest; where gold's volatility is about 12 per cent a year, silver's is around 25 per cent. A 10 or even 20-cent overnight move in the silver price is not unusual—a large move in something priced at $5.

Base metals: Copper, Aluminium, Lead, Zinc, Nickel, Tin

Australia is a major producer of aluminium, copper, zinc, lead, nickel and tin, the diverse group known as 'base metals'. Each differs from the other by as much as base metals in general differ from gold, but for ease of discussion they are grouped under the one heading.

A vital difference between the markets in base metals and the gold market is that there is no stockpile in base metals, ie, there is no equivalent of the central banks' vaults of gold. The base metals market is driven by the forces of supply and demand. Aluminium and copper would lead the way in terms of long-term liquidity, with zinc next. Consumers and producers interact to create a two-way market that does not exist in gold. Whereas the forward price in gold reflects an interest-rate differential between the cost of borrowing gold and money-market interest rates, the forward prices of base metals are driven by conditions in the physical market and, in the 1990s, also by fund investments and speculation. And the physical market might be fundamentally strong but in the short-term conditions could be affected by, say, a big selling order on the futures market.

Another distinction between bullion and base metals is that gold is nearly always in contango, with forward prices higher than the spot price, whereas base metals are frequently in the reverse, backwardation, with forward prices lower than spot. This creates a difficulty for producers who might be faced with attractive spot prices but have no production to sell for perhaps eighteen months, by which time prices may have fallen. Producers work around this by using forwards or *curve locks* (the base metals market's term for interest-rate swaps) which may enable them to carry forward the higher spot prices, or at least reduce the backwardation. For consumers buying forward, backwardation is very convenient.

Hedging activity in base metals is expected to rival that in energy in the second half of the 1990s, a view boosted, by late 1994, by a two-year high in base metals prices—levels that producers would like to lock in. Further, prices of some metals, such as copper, were very volatile in the second half of 1994 and volatility encourages more operators to hedge. However, even worldwide activity in base metals is restricted to a handful of banks specialising in the area. Most activity takes place in the London and New York time-zones, with base metals priced off the quotes on the London Metals Exchange (LME).

That prices are set in the northern hemisphere for metals produced in the southern—not only Australia but Malaysia, Indonesia and Chile are major exporters of base metals—is a historical accident dating from the days when Britain was a trading powerhouse importing metals for use in its booming industries. For example, the three-month copper and tin contracts traded on the LME were pitched to match the time it took to ship copper from Chile or tin from Malaysia. Modern communications technology now enables banks in the southern hemisphere to take a greater role in base metals pricing, filling a gap in the time-zone between the US and European markets.

Considerable momentum is being created by Australian financial institutions which see a chance to develop hedging business by replicating in base metals what has been achieved in gold. The emergence of US fund managers as investors in base metals has helped bring the sector into the limelight. While producers have in general established good relationships and hedging facilities with the major markets in the northern hemisphere, a small group of intermediaries is carving out a niche in Australia, offering a growing range of commodity-linked financing facilities, such as copper loans (similar to gold loans) and metals-based note issues which enable an investor to buy a right to be repaid in a quantity of base metals or underlying currency. Metals-based notes are similar to long-dated call options, with the investor taking a reduction in yield which covers the cost of buying a call option over the metal. Many producers find comfort in having market-making services in Australia and the possibility of a relationship with an institution that can explain a complex financial structure face-to-face rather than over the phone. LME brokers, conscious that banks have the edge over them in terms of capital and credit-standing, are happy to see banks offering over-the-counter facilities and then in turn use the LME market to hedge. For many producers it makes sense, from a cost standpoint, to deal through an Australian institution rather than direct with overseas markets.

Market-making in base metals in Australia is less developed than in the gold market and certainly is in fewer hands; liquidity in the time-zone is increasing but is still centred in London. Essentially, base metals activity in Australia in the mid-1990s is similar to that in gold in the early 1980s, when liquidity in the time-zone was still to grow. Copper is the most actively traded and very volatile; aluminium, of which Australia is a major producer, offers good liquidity, followed by zinc, nickel, tin. Liquidity in lead is poor. But given the trade in base metals between Australia and countries such as Japan, China and South Korea, which are big consumers of aluminium, copper and zinc, there is good reason to believe that expectations of growth in base metals hedging are soundly based. Moreover, whereas the gold market tends to be one-sided in the sense that producers hedge but consumers do not, in many base metals, especially copper, the market is two-sided with both producers and con-sumers hedging. Gold, on the other hand, attracts a speculative interest that is not prominent in base metals.

Those who see a big future in base metals hedging cite the example of oil, where hedging is now big business because oil costs are a major financial risk for, say, transport companies. If aluminium is a big part of a company's production costs, then it makes sense to hedge aluminium costs and budget around that. For example, a car manufacturer hedges aluminium.

Most hedging products offered in foreign exchange and gold markets are available in base metals, with the exception of spot-deferred, which would be difficult because of the volatility in the spot price of base metals (base metals' spot prices are more volatile than their forward prices) and the tendency for the market to slip into backwardation. Forwards and options are used out to five years. Reflecting the thinner market, term deals vary from base metal to base metal; for example, the market in nickel is thin beyond eighteen months and copper starts to struggle beyond two years.

SOFT COMMODITIES

Wool

Australia is the world's largest producer and exporter of wool. In June 1994 the Sydney Futures Exchange announced that it was proceeding in 1995 with a deliverable wool futures contract. The move was of particular sentimental relevance for the SFE, which began life in 1960 as the Sydney Greasy Wool Futures Exchange, trading contracts based on the greasy wool equivalent of 3 000lb of clean wool. Wool, Australia's third-largest export, enjoyed a boom until the early 1970s, when its price collapsed. But it was the introduction of a wool floor price in 1972 that, by removing the need to hedge, dealt a lethal blow to wool futures. While diversifying into other areas to broaden its base, the SFE in 1977 also phased out trading in greasy wool futures and introduced a contract based on micron wool, taking into account the changing structure of the wool trade and its increasing reliance on micron wool as the price determinant.

The wool contract remained physically deliverable until 1986, when it became cash-settled. Hopes that removing the obligation to deliver would broaden the range of users of the contract were unfulfilled. The wool futures contract, although virtually dormant, remained listed. Then in February 1991 the reserve price scheme was suspended, raising the possibility of reviving wool futures trading.

Several parties were highly supportive of a new wool contract, notably Wool International, a government body that grew out of the former Australian Wool Corporation and was initially known as the Australian Wool Realisation Commission. Wool International was charged with reducing the stockpile that had accumulated and, as a related task, to establish forward-trading instruments which would facilitate this reduction as well as encourage forward trading by woolgrowers. While the wool industry remained as diverse in views as it had ever been, with the preference of Wool International for a deliverable contract not always matching those of the woolgrowers, buyers or selling brokers, there was also strong support for a viable futures contract from several specialist banks and wool-selling houses.

Backed by such widespread support, the SFE was enthusiastic about seeing a new contract established. However, experience had taught the exchange that designing a new contract would only be one element in reviving wool futures trading. Price and information dissemination is also important. And for a deliverable contract it is extremely important that the wool be independently appraised and certified; a successful futures market relies on giving delivery from seller to buyer of a standard quality and standard description which is acceptable to both and guaranteed by the clearing house (no easy matter, given the hundreds of different types of wool). The contract specifies acceptable weight, fibre diameter, vegetable matter, length, strength, colour and topmaking style.

The new contract is deliverable, held in many quarters to be more efficient than a cash-settled contract because it is said to create more interaction between the cash and futures market and enhances price discovery by providing a daily indicator of wool prices. An opposing view is that a cash-settled contract would be preferable, given that the wool industry has benchmark prices established at regular auctions which virtually provide a daily price. Also, in view of the Australian market's geographical spread, a potential difficulty arises with delivery possibly being taken in different centres such as Brisbane, Sydney and Adelaide. This raises concerns about significant variations in wool quality between centres and between seasons.

The contract introduced on the SFE is based on 21-micron wool, although it also allows delivery of wool that is finer or coarser by 1.5 microns, which will carry a premium or a discount to par. Wool finer than 21 microns is in demand by fashion houses and sells at a premium, particularly in the Asian markets which demand 'cool' wool. A 21-micron wool contract was favoured by the wool-buyers, woolbrokers and the mills; Wool International, which owns the stockpile, and the growers tended to favour 22-micron (the bulk of the stockpile is in 22–23 micron). In the SFE's view setting the contract at 21 microns should enable most growers to hedge adequately; those most exposed to basis risk will be those growing, say, less than 19-micron or greater than 23-micron wool. Basis risk, the risk of divergence between prices in futures and prices in the physical market, is an integral element of futures trading, irrespective of the contract's base. Those in favour of a 22-micron standard point to the greater volatility in the finer wools.

Growers facing the greater basis risk will be able to tailor their hedging requirements with a bank or wool-broker, execute an over-the-counter transaction with them and let the expert handle the risk. Given the price difference between the various microns, the ability to hedge through basis contracts offered over-the-counter by, say, Elders Risk Management, will further enable growers to manage price risk.

However, experience has shown that demand for the wool contract is unlikely to come largely from the growers. While the growers might generate some OTC deals with banks and brokers, the backbone of support for wool futures will come from traditional users such as G.H. Michell & Sons, Australia's largest wool processors, the large wool-selling brokers Elders Ltd and Wesfarmers Dalgety Ltd, Prouvost et Lefebvre, the Australian trading division of the French textile company Chargeurs, the Japanese wool-buying houses Itochu, Kanematsu and Marubeni, which forward-sell to the mills, and the mills themselves, being the end-users taking stock forward. In the heyday of the earlier wool futures trading, more than 80 per cent of turnover was generated by wool-buying houses and mills. Between 1960 and 1972, from the start of wool futures on the Sydney Greasy Wool Futures Exchange to the establishment of the Australian Wool Corporation's reserve price scheme, no more than 5 per cent of the exchange's turnover resulted from hedging by woolgrowers. Growers favour options and over-the-counter forward contracts as a way of managing risk that locks in a price and avoids margin calls. Banks for their part like the idea of growers covering their risk which in turn should mean growers would be able to achieve finance at better terms.

Example of simple hedge using wool futures

Date	Cash	Futures
February	Plans to sell wool at auction in October	Sells October futures at 800 cents/kg
October	Sells wool at auction and receives 700 cents/kg	Buys October futures at 710 cents/kg
Auction price	700 cents a kg	
Plus futures profit	90 cents a kg (800 less 710)	
Total price	790 cents a kg	
Less futures brokerage, say	2 cents a kg	
Net price	788 cents a kg	

Prices in the cash market have fallen between February and October but by selling forward through futures the producer has locked in a profit. Had prices risen in the intervening period the profit made in the physical market would have offset (even outweighed) the costs of the hedge.

Cotton

Australia, ranked about fourth-largest exporter of cotton, producing some 10 per cent of the world's exportable cotton, sells around 90 per cent of its crop overseas. The benchmark price for the global cotton market is the New York Cotton Exchange's No 2 futures contract. With cotton sold internationally in $US, Australian producers can either sell cotton in $US or $A. Where cotton is sold in $US, the Australian producer is vulnerable to fluctuations in the $US/$A exchange rate and so exchange-rate risk is an important component of cotton prices which has to be hedged. However, when hedging exchange-rate risk, a cotton producer will consider expected cashflow, budget, interest-rate differentials and currency levels.

Cotton marketing groups such as Namoi Cotton, Queensland Cotton, Cotton Trading Corporation and Colly Farms Cotton Ltd compete to buy cotton from the growers and, to win the business, offer a range of marketing and hedging products. The merchants undertake hedging which provides an $A price for the risk-averse growers.

If forward prices are attractive to them, Australian cotton growers will want to lock in prices further forward than the mills are prepared to buy, so the cotton cooperatives/merchants intermediate between the two. Growers are normally offered prices as far forward as two years, but they will sell forward only if the price suits. The merchants (unless they have offsetting forward physical sales on their books) then lay off their risk on the New York Cotton Exchange's futures and option contracts, a highly liquid market which attracts considerable speculative interest.

Growers use the hedging facilities offered by merchants to hedge future and foreign-exchange risk without locking in the basis, ie, the difference in the price of Australian cotton and that of cotton on the NY exchange. Until a grower is confident of producing the cotton, he or she will prefer to commit only to a financial transaction that can be unwound (eg, an option that involves only the payment of an upfront premium) should cotton production fall short. Merchants appear to fulfil a brokerage role for the growers, enabling them to hedge financial exposure, but with the obligation on the part of the grower to deliver cotton at some stage. Once a grower is confident of cotton production, he or she can lock in the last leg, ie, the basis.

The merchants also place orders on the New York exchange on behalf of the growers. Modern communications technology enables the growers, if they wish, to handle their own foreign-exchange and commodity hedging. The larger growers operate their own accounts directly with futures brokers; however, smaller growers are more comfortable going through merchants who can package foreign-exchange and commodity risk and achieve better pricing than could a small operator acting independently.

An over-the-counter market in derivatives for the cotton industry is developing in Australia with a few banks which specialise in commodity-linked derivatives offering OTC options and swaps. Rothschild Australia is developing OTC options based on a formula of futures and currency prices that will enable it to offer $A-denominated options to growers. An inhibiting feature for that market, though, is the absence of a level of liquidity that ensures a bank can offset its risk. A factor acting against cotton is that it is not a widely traded, 24-hour liquid product; rather, it tends to be handled by a select few specialists. In terms of price discovery and hedging, though, the market is well developed in Australia. It is free of government regulation and cotton business is aggressively pursued by some ten merchants working with a well-educated clientele, hedging not just their cotton but also their currency and interest-rate exposures.

A drawback for Australian users of the New York futures market is that they cannot deliver but have to cash-settle their futures contracts, whereas the US merchants can deliver. Also, US import bans prevent them from selling cotton into that market, so Australian participants in New York futures are left with some basis risk. While Australian cash prices for cotton have a strong correlation with prices on the NY Cotton Exchange, the basis risk is greater for Australian cotton vis-a-vis the New York market than it is for the various types of US cotton. Exacerbating basis risk is the likelihood that specific US conditions could influence the cotton price; for example, the US market could be suffering a shortage of cotton while the rest of the world enjoys good supply, but the US supply problem would show up in the futures price which the rest of the world uses as its benchmark.

Wheat

Australia, one of the world's major exporters of wheat, sells about 70 per cent of its wheat crop overseas, a volume that accounts for some 11 per cent of the world market. The Australian Wheat Board (AWB) is the sole exporter of Australian wheat and generally hedges up to around 25 per cent of the wheat crop at any one time. Liquidity problems prevent the AWB from establishing larger positions (see below). When growers deliver wheat to the AWB pool they receive the average sales price for pool wheat, net of marketing and finance costs. The price the growers receive is a reflection of prevailing prices on the international market, which emphasises the extent to which Australian wheat farmers are exposed to fluctuating overseas prices. (This point was driven home in 1990/91 when wheat prices crashed, only a year after the AWB removed the guaranteed minimum price to growers which had been in place since 1939.) Because most sales are made after the wheat is delivered, growers receive a percentage of the estimated value of their crop on delivery and then a series of payments until sales are completed and pool returns finalised. Growers who deliver to a pool have a continuing exposure to the market as part of a pool.

Part of the AWB's charter is to manage risk on behalf of the growers. The 1989 Wheat Marketing Bill stated the AWB's objectives:

> to maximise the net returns to Australian wheat growers who sell pool return wheat to the AWB by securing, developing and maintaining markets for wheat and for wheat products and by minimising costs as far as possible;

> by participating, in a commercial manner, in the market for wheat and wheat products, to provide Australian wheat growers with a choice of marketing options.

To this end, the AWB hedges wheat using futures and options on the Chicago Board of Trade, the world's largest grain exchange, and on the Kansas City Board of Trade and the

Minneapolis Grain Exchange. The AWB's hedging program is handled by its New York office, established in the early 1980s. Exchange-related business accounts for about 80 per cent of AWB's hedging, with an increasing proportion carried out using over-the-counter facilities. The board creates cover in other ways, such as encouraging customers to buy wheat forward and build risk management into their pricing.

AWB faces considerable basis risk in hedging on CBOT because the exchange's contract is based on deliverable US wheat, leaving non-US users of the contract exposed to local supply-and-demand factors which affect the price of US wheat and consequently the price of the futures contract. For example, the US uses direct subsidies to push export sales of wheat and to stimulate domestic demand. To provide some diversification from the US markets and to help with basis risk, the AWB hedges against French wheat using over-the-counter facilities (in the absence of a French wheat futures contract). French wheat swaps provide exposure to European Community price movements and thus further diversification.

The trend towards the AWB using an increasing amount of OTC products reflects the greater flexibility they provide and the liquidity problems that arise from time to time on the futures market. Open interest on the CBOT fluctuates so that at times the AWB—one of the exchange's largest customers—could have an exposure which is enormous relative to the size of the market. Because of this the Commodity Futures Trading Commission (CFTC) imposes a 'hedge-and-spec' limit on AWB futures activity which inhibits the AWB from hedging 100 per cent of the wheat crop on the exchange.

Wheat, being a staple food product, is subject to considerable political influence on its price. However, it is expected that international demand for risk management in wheat will grow as countries progressively remove regulations on the market. In Australia a number of wheat farmers have grouped together to trade Chicago wheat options, raising the question of the practicality of individual growers hedging their own wheat. While it is conceivable that in the years ahead the AWB may face competition in exporting and hedging, market conditions make life tough for individual hedgers, specifically the world wheat market's susceptibility to interference and the existence of basis risk between Australian and US wheat prices. This differential can at times be more volatile than the price of wheat, making hedging very risky, even inadvisable.

Sugar

Sugar is Australia's second-largest export crop and Queensland's second largest rural commodity. Almost 80 per cent of Queensland's output is exported. The Queensland Sugar Corporation (QSC), formed in 1991, acquires raw sugar by legislation and is a monopoly seller of sugar produced in Queensland. QSC is the world's largest exporter of raw sugar and is responsible for selling about 95 per cent of Australian production, with CSR engaged as marketing export agent.

Queensland Sugar Corporation hedges about 60 to 70 per cent of sugar production, using futures contracts and exchange-traded options available on the New York Coffee, Sugar and Cocoa Exchange, one of the largest futures exchanges, whose sugar contract is the world benchmark. Because the sugar contract traded on the New York exchange is *the* world sugar contract there is no basis risk involved. However, with most of Queensland's raw sugar sales priced against the US futures contract, the revenue of growers and millers is highly exposed to world developments. And with almost all sugar sales, domestically and overseas, denominated in $US, Queensland Sugar Corporation is exposed to the $A/$US exchange rate and so has to manage currency as well as sugar-price risk.

An average break-up of Queensland Sugar Corporation's hedging activities would be: 60 per cent in exchange-traded futures and options on the New York Coffee, Sugar and Cocoa Exchange; 20 per cent in long-term contracts for a fixed price and fixed quantity and generally for terms of between two and five years; 15 per cent in fixed-price and fixed-quantity sales generally for terms of less than two years; and 5 per cent in over-the-counter arrangements with trade houses, customers and financial institutions.

ENERGY PRODUCTS

It is not hard to identify companies with exposure to energy risks, considering the variety of companies that use different types of machinery reliant on oil, gas and electricity. The end-users of oil and energy derivatives in Australia would be the major shipping lines, airlines and transport companies which consume oil and so hedge their fuel costs. The Australian refiners tend to leave hedging to their multinational parents.

Oil

Oil prices can be extremely volatile, forcing attention on to managing oil-price risk for oil producers and consumers. The six-month Kuwait crisis which began in August 1990 and culminated in the Gulf War in January 1991 caused a steep rise in oil costs which sparked a rush of operators into oil swaps; however, business contracted as the crisis receded. Excluding that period, the volatility of oil prices between 1989 and 1994 was 22 per cent, nearly double the volatility seen in the $A/$US exchange rate over the same period. Such unpredictable movements have encouraged an increase in the range of oil-price hedging techniques, which include products that fix forward prices and option-based arrangements which set a floor price but enable the hedger also to benefit from a favourable move.

The oil market centres mostly on the New York time-zone but some Australian intermediaries quote oil prices for clients and several banks run large energy books out of Singapore which would be coordinated with their bank's global book. Tapis, a light Malaysian crude oil, is the most relevant for the Asian and Australian markets, and several operators make markets in Tapis and offer Tapis swaps.

The oil market quotes several different indexes. West Texas Intermediate (WTI) crude oil, listed on Nymex (New York Mercantile Exchange), is regarded as the benchmark indicator of world oil prices. Other oils quoted include Brent (North Sea oil), quoted on London's International Petroleum Exchange, Tapis, bunker fuel, jet fuel, gasoil (similar to diesel oil) and so on. WTI and Tapis are the two main barometers for oil in the Australian/Asia–Pacific region and the recent development of Tapis swaps and options is of particular benefit to the Australasian markets. However, WTI and Tapis are quite separate markets which do not move in tandem; Tapis, less freely traded than WTI, is less of an indicator of world supply-and-demand factors than its more widely traded US counterpart. Rather, Tapis reflects supply and demand in the Asian region. These features result in there being a price difference between the two of as much as $3 a barrel. There is a need for an exchange-traded product to cater for the heightened activity in oil and the frequently large basis risk between Tapis and WTI.

The Sydney Futures Exchange has forged a trading link with Nymex placing Nymex's WTI oil futures and option contracts in the Asia–Pacific time-zone and opening up a 24-hour market in oil. Founded in 1872 as the Butter and Cheese Exchange, Nymex was renamed the New York Mercantile Exchange in 1882 and was the first futures exchange to introduce energy contracts. It has emerged as world leader in trading energy futures and options, accounting for some 80 per cent of world energy futures trading. In 1993 Nymex adopted an electronic screen-dealing system based on the SFE's Sycom and it is through Nymex's version of Sycom, known as Access, that SFE members can trade Nymex's energy products. Under the terms of the agreement SFE members can trade Nymex products based on heating oil, gasoline, natural gas and platinum, in addition to the benchmark WTI crude oil futures.

Products for managing oil-price risk include:

Futures, offering exchange-traded contracts which enable a hedger to buy or sell a standardised product at a specified future date. The largest crude oil futures market is the WTI contract traded on Nymex and, from 1995, available to SFE members through Sycom. Brent, traded on the International Petroleum Exchange in London, is another.

Swaps, which are traded over-the-counter, as are interest-rate and currency swaps, with the most common for oil being a fixed-price swap. This enables a producer to receive a fixed price for a barrel of a specified type of oil and in return pay a floating price set according to a market index. A relevant development for the Australian market is the rise in the availability of Tapis swaps, which are quoted out to two years and longer if necessary. Swaps prices in $US per barrel give the fixed price that an intermediary would pay a producer in return for a floating payment over the same period. The floating index generally used is the APPI (Asian Petroleum Price Index) Tapis price published every Thursday, averaged over a month or quarter. At the end of the swap period the producer either makes or receives a payment, depending on the movement in the floating price. The swap market has reasonable depths, with quotes available out to five, even ten, years.

Options, which provide the right, but not the obligation, to buy or sell at a predetermined price. As with other types of options, a buyer of an oil option limits the downside risk by paying a premium but does not limit his or her potential to gain from a favourable movement in price. Options over Tapis are providing additional flexibility for Australasian markets. Oil options are Asian-style which tend to be cheaper because the option's settlement value is based on the difference between the strike price and the average price of the underlying commodity during the life of the option (see 'Learning the Language').

Swaptions, collars and *exotic options*—all variations of the above (see 'Learning the Language').

Example of an oil hedge

A producer enters into a Tapis swap in December 1994 to receive a fixed price for the second quarter in 1995 against monthly settlements in April, May and June. The swap price for second quarter 1995 is $US20 a barrel. If, at the end of April 1995, the average price of the APPI quotes during the month were $US18, the intermediary would make a payment of $2 a barrel to the producer. If the price were $US21 a barrel then the producer would pay $US1 a barrel. Either way, the producer has secured a known price of $US20 a barrel.

A producer might chose to buy a Tapis put option at $US20, providing the right but not the obligation to sell Tapis to the intermediary at $US20 (cash-settlement only). The producer would exercise this right if Tapis prices were below $US20. If the oil price were $US19 the producer would receive $US1 a barrel; if the price were $US21 then the producer would let the option expire. The producer has to factor the cost of the option premium into any gain made.

Gas

Australia is self-sufficient in natural gas and has vast reserves available for export. Supplies from the Cooper Basin in South Australia, discovered in the 1960s, provide about 40 per cent of the country's needs through a network of underground pipelines to Sydney and other cities. Other major gas fields are the Bass Strait, the North-West Shelf and the Surat-Bowen basin.

Natural gas involves high development costs and long lead times between finding the gas and selling it to a large distributor such as Australian Gas Light Company in NSW or Gas and Fuel Corporation in Victoria. The companies searching for and developing gas operate with fixed-price contracts, negotiated between, say, AGL and producers, with a percentage linked to the Consumer Price Index.

It is likely that the gas market will be broken up to increase competition and that tranches of gas will be bought and sold. This would in turn give rise to the use of hedging techniques based on swaps, options and forwards.

At present, gas in Australia is sold on a state basis within each of the six states and cross-border gas sales are not made. Given that the market operates with a fixed price, it is not yet possible to treat gas as a tradeable commodity as it is in, say, North America where gas is traded spot, forward and stored. The freer US market has given rise to substantial activity in natural gas swaps. However, the trend in Australia towards national competition, evidenced in the electricity market and the establishment of the national electricity distribution grid, is having an impact on the gas market.

Electricity

There is no market for electricity swaps or other derivatives in Australia because electricity is available under a bulk supply tariff. However, that could well change as the industry moves to a more market-based system.

In New Zealand developments are well under way towards establishing a competitive spot market, and exchange-traded and over-the-counter derivatives markets in electricity. This process began with the deregulation of the retail energy sector, which saw the privatisation of the former power companies and the emergence of a mix of publicly-listed and trust-owned companies. Many companies have joined to form common electricity-trading enterprises as the old geographical franchises disappeared. Major companies, such as BP, and nationwide groups of schools, have taken out contracts with single electricity companies to supply their power requirements.

The wholesale market has also been reformed, ahead of a change in the shape of the monopoly generator, Electricity Corporation of New Zealand (ECNZ). The national grid operator, Trans Power, was separated from ECNZ in July 1994, and major independent generating competition is on the horizon.

In 1993 the Electricity Market Company (EMCO) was established to develop the necessary framework for wholesale markets and to foster methods for trading electricity and related financial risk-management products. Trading in wholesale electricity products began in July 1994 on the New Zealand Electricity Market (NZEM), an umbrella term for markets operated by EMCO, with secondary trading of one-year hedging facilities sold by ECNZ. This was the first step in developing futures trading in wholesale electricity. All trading on NZEM is executed on-line through an automated system, COMIT (Commodity Market Information and Trading system).

CHAPTER 8
· ·
REPOS (REPURCHASE AGREEMENTS)

The explosion in derivatives trading over the past few years has helped fuel an upsurge in activity in repurchase agreements. This reflects the role these instruments play in providing major derivatives traders with an avenue for funding when they are long physical stock (ie, they are holding bonds) and with a way of gaining access to physical stock when they need to cover a short (sold) position. Repurchase agreements have become useful tools for those managing swap portfolios.

A repurchase agreement (repo or RP) is a series of transactions involving the sale of a security and the simultaneous agreement to buy it back, on an agreed date and at an agreed price. A repo gives the holder title to the security; it is not a secured loan.

Repos can be 'open-ended', ie, executed on demand, or overnight or for a fixed term. Generally, they are arranged for periods ranging between one day and three months, with most having maturities of two months or less.

REPOS AND THE RESERVE BANK

Repurchase agreements are a key tool of the Reserve Bank's liquidity-management operations in the market. The bank also makes outright purchases and sales of commonwealth government securities but, when undertaken for liquidity-management purposes, these are restricted to short-term securities. Securities used in repos can be of longer maturities, and their term is not related to the maturity of the repo agreement. This enables the Reserve Bank to use a far wider range of securities; for example, a repo in long-term bonds can be used to achieve the same impact on liquidity in the cash market as an outright transaction in short-term treasury notes.

The Reserve Bank's transactions in repos and shorter-term commonwealth government securities (up to one year in maturity) are carried out with the authorised money-market dealers. These transactions are settled on a same-day basis, ie, value is given and received within the day, and so affect the dealers' demand for cash in the market that day.

In the wider market, repos—also known as buy-backs, sell-backs and reciprocal purchase agreements—can involve other securities, such as state government bonds, as agreed by the parties to the repo.

Repurchase agreements have enjoyed a surge in popularity in recent years but are not a recent phenomenon. A form of repos dates from the 1950s and the beginnings of the 'official' short-term money market, when a number of stockbrokers began 'buy-back' activities in government securities. By 1954 the stockbrokers had begun to offer clients facilities for investing temporary surpluses of cash. The brokers sold government bonds to the clients and the parties agreed that the brokers would buy the bonds back at a future date and at a set price. In effect, the brokers were borrowing their clients' funds and securing the borrowings with government bonds. The clients were lending funds (investing) and taking the bonds as security. Such clients would probably have willingly bought government bonds had they been certain about the length of time they could afford to invest but they were reluctant to buy bonds outright in case they had to sell them within a short time, possibly at a loss. Short-dated government securities at that time were not available in sufficient quantity to guarantee a thriving market, nor was there much secondary-market trading. With the brokers' methods, funds were on loan for short periods, from a few days to one month.

In *In Reserve—Central Banking in Australia 1945–75*, Professor Boris Schedvin records that, by the late 1950s, 'there were . . .

distinct signs that the market in government securities was increasing in sophistication'.

> Early in 1957 the [central] Bank was approached by the ES&A to enquire whether a buy-back arrangement in relation to government securities would be considered. Such an arrangement was advantageous to an institution with excess short-term liquidity because it obtained 3 per cent on money that otherwise would have been idle. The offer was accepted, the Board approved the arrangement in February 1957, and during the year the Bank entered into a small number of repurchase agreements amounting to about $27 million.

Buy-back activity was given a fresh lease of life, although in a different form, when, in August 1984, the Reserve Bank announced the introduction of repurchase agreements in commonwealth government securities between itself and the authorised money-market dealers. With treasury notes in short supply, and the Reserve Bank keen to ensure sufficient liquidity was available to the market, repos provided a useful way of liquefying longer-term bonds. Repo activity rose significantly after August 1986, following a Reserve Bank decision to allow authorised dealers to buy and sell securities under repo with banks and other clients. Repos provide the central bank with additional flexibility in liquidity management and, in recent years, have come to constitute the bulk of the Reserve Bank's open-market operations. Under these arrangements, when the central bank offers a 'buy repo' it buys stock on a deficit day (a day on which there is a shortfall of cash, so the central bank puts cash into the banking system), and agrees to sell that stock back (taking cash out of the system) on a day when there is expected to be a surplus of funds. 'Sell repos' have the reverse effect.

Repos are useful in repositioning funds and help reduce day-to-day fluctuations in the level of cash in the system. When the Reserve Bank is offering to buy repos, ie, putting funds into the system, it takes into account the liquidity effects of unwinding the repo (which takes funds out of the system) when selecting between repos of different terms. Rates set on repos are related to the prevailing cash rates in the market, not the yields on the underlying securities. When buying repos, the

Reserve Bank sorts the bids into descending order of yield (the bank is looking to provide funds at the highest), and into maturities. When selling repos, the Reserve Bank, being effectively a borrower, sorts the bids into ascending order of yield. However, in most instances maturity is a more important consideration than price.

REPOS AND THE MARKET

In recent years the repo market has expanded enormously. It is impossible to gauge an accurate turnover figure (because of the difficulties of determining whether a deal is matched, inter-principal or dealt through a series of intermediaries) but it is estimated that annual turnover could exceed $2 trillion—making the repo market the largest in Australia in terms of turnover. Repos account for about 90 per cent of authorised dealers' open-market transactions with the RBA, although that proportion varies from dealer to dealer. A huge amount of repo business is carried out by the major market-makers in fixed-interest securities (banks and investment banks).

The stocklending facilities provided by state government borrowers such as NSW TCorp and Queensland Treasury Corporation, in furnishing an additional port-of-call for those in need of stock, have deepened market liquidity by fostering market-making, and so contribute to increased activity in repos.

USERS OF REPOS

Repos are bought and sold for a number of reasons. They offer a way to obtain otherwise scarce stock. Further, they foster market-making in commonwealth bonds and semi-government securities by providing an extra dimension of flexibility in turning over stock.

Sellers of repos

At its most straightforward, a seller of repos gains short-term liquidity at an attractive rate.

Typically, a seller of repos could be a party which is a natural holder of stock—an institutional investor whose business includes holding bonds or a dealer holding securities as part of his or her stock-in-trade—and is looking to gross up his or her portfolio by selling the stock under repo at a cash rate below that at which the proceeds can be reinvested. For example, assume that a fund manager (natural holder of several hundred million dollars' worth of bonds) has stock that is keenly sought by traders who are short of the stock; the fund manager sells the stock under repo at a cash rate of, say, 6.25 per cent, then reinvests the proceeds in the cash market at 6.50 per cent, realising a 25-basis point profit.

A seller might also be a trading house or investment bank which has taken a position in bonds that has to be funded—but does not operate with a deposit base so it borrows the cash it needs by putting stock out on repo. Or a bank might sell a repo as an alternative to raising deposits in the wholesale market; it can fund its bond position through the repo market.

Buyers of repos

On the other side are the buyers—investors keen to place cash through repos because that offers top-class security. Most, though not all, repos are based on commonwealth or semi-government bonds and so carry minimum credit risk. (A small proportion of repo activity is based on corporate bonds.)

Someone with a short position in bonds would buy securities under a repo to cover that position. Option trading and derivatives in general also spur activity in repos because they increase the need for hedging positions through selling short physical bonds. For example, a trader has bought a put option and sold securities against it as a hedge; he or she would buy stock under a repo to cover that short position.

A bank buyer of securities under a repo could obtain stock to satisfy PAR (prime assets ratio) requirements, for example by buying commonwealth government securities on a short-term basis through the repo market in preference to buying long-dated securities, resulting in considerably less exposure to movements in interest rates.

REPOS AND SECURITIES LENDING

Activity in securities lending has increased significantly around the world in recent years, often associated with equities but also with fixed-interest securities. Securities lending in Australia dates from 1984 and the creation of the reporting bond-dealers, which were a considerable catalyst to market-making. A pioneer in the area was The Bond Lending Company, established in 1984 by Australian Gilt Securities as a special-purpose company focusing on fostering trading in bonds. The volume of activity in securities lending—transacted between professional trader and institutional client or between institutions—is considerably lower than that of repos but securities lending business generates stock for the repo market (the preserve of the professional traders).

Several institutions prefer to *lend* their securities rather than execute a repo. Securities lending, carried out for a fee, is a borrowing-lending exercise that does not require any movement of cash; the lender of the stock is paid a fee by the borrower who also provides the lender with 'substock' (substitution stock). A repo, on the other hand, is a buy-sell transaction where the cash value of the securities changes hands, giving operators potentially large cashflows to reinvest. There is a degree of uncertainty associated with the reinvestment rate and an element of credit risk on the reinvestment.

Securities lending does not offer the opportunity to arbitrage the cash spread that is available through a repo. However, many non-professional operators prefer securities lending because it does not generate cash that has to be reinvested in the market and is a simpler process to administer because it eliminates tax and accrual complications. Also, the mark-to-market risk associated with securities lending is minimal because bond-holders have 'swapped' stock whose yields, even with a major market move, will shift in tandem.

From a practical point of view, notional ownership of stock changes hands with securities lending, because the two main settlement systems, RITS and Austraclear, can only handle buy-and-sell (not lending) transactions. So for the purposes of settlement a transaction is processed as a buy-sell, irrespective of its being a securities loan or a repo.

Mechanics of a repo

The mechanics of a repo in which the Reserve Bank sells a repo and an authorised dealer purchases it (the deal could be transacted between any two parties as buyer and seller, eg bond dealer and client):

The Reserve Bank sells a repo of $20 million of commonwealth government securities with a 12.5 per cent coupon, maturing September 1997, and a market yield of 9.95 per cent. The RBA repos the stock for three days, say, 9 to 12 December, at a rate of 6.30 per cent. The price of the securities is $108.932 per $100 face value, $21 786 400 for $20 million.

Figure 8.1   Example of a repurchase agreement

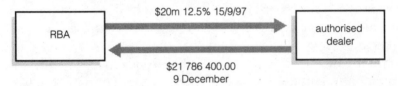

The transaction is reversed on 12 December. Through RITS, the securities are transferred back to the original seller (in this case the Reserve Bank), which in return credits the authorised dealer's account with $21 786 400.00 plus interest at 6.30 per cent per annum for three days. The authorised dealer has earned $11 281.18 in interest.

Figure 8.2   Example of a reversal of a repurchase agreement

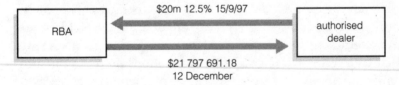

PRICE OF REPO

The price of a repo, in terms of the premium/discount to the cash rate, varies depending on the demand for, or supply of, the underlying stock. If the stock is in plentiful supply and regularly issued, the premium is low, eg, a repo would be transacted at about 5.85 per cent against a cash rate of 6 per cent. If the stock were very actively traded and in short supply the premium would be higher, with a repo trading as high as 5.3 per cent against a cash rate of 6 per cent.

MARKET RISK

A repo with a maturity of more than one day involves a potential risk of a change in the market value of the relevant securities (which are owned for the time being by a purchaser of a repo). Exposure can be limited by marking the security to market at regular intervals. The market value of the repo is sometimes altered, by mutual agreement, to reflect a change in the yield of the securities—for example, where a repo has been transacted at a yield of 9 per cent and a cash rate of 6.30 per cent but the market moves to 10 per cent so that the stock's market value has been reduced. Variations are mutually agreed and validated with a confirmation-of-variation letter. While the market value of the repo is sometimes changed, the face value and the repo rate remain unaltered. When a change in market value occurs, the repo is marked to market, which entails settling on the sell-buy leg and starting it again at the new market yield. Interest accrues again from that point.

SETTLEMENT

Repos may be settled through RITS or Austraclear. Commonwealth government securities are settled through RITS, while semi-government and most other money-market securities are settled through Austraclear. With transactions involving institutions or corporate clients which are not members of RITS or Austraclear, settlement involves the physical exchange of securities and bank cheques.

Repo settlement or securities lending transactions look like outright purchases or sales, except that in RITS the transaction can be flagged as a repo for statistical purposes (although many participants do not do so).

See chapter 12 for documentation of repos.

Part II

....

Risks, management and controls

CHAPTER 9
....

RISKS ASSOCIATED WITH
DERIVATIVES: CASE STUDIES

*Several of the problems exhibited by the markets are common to new
activities: data on many areas are lacking (with opacity reinforced by
the off-balance-sheet nature of the derivatives); market practices,
including documentation, are often not standardised; some areas of
the law are untested; the markets can be shallow and volatile; management of risk may lag behind product innovation; and the requisite
skills are not widely spread.* Bank of England 1993.

BARINGS PLC

The futures-trading-related collapse of the 233-year-old small
but prestige British investment bank, Barings PLC, in February
1995, coming as it did on the heels of a string of derivatives-
associated corporate losses, shook the world's financial markets.
The episode raised more questions than it answered, foremost
among them being how a respected institution with a trading
history stretching back to 1762 could fail in its supervision and
control of an offshore office to the extent that a trader could
rack up losses of more than $US1 billion ($A1.35 billion) that
wiped out the bank's capital and reserves.

Even as the details of the trading strategy that led to the
losses were still being revealed, one message stood out loud and
clear. Barings had failed to implement the most basic of checks
and balances essential in any treasury-dealing operation, large
or small, bank or a corporate: to segregate the duties of trading

and settlement. The losses were the consequence of large positions, estimated around $US27 billion, taken in the Nikkei 225 futures contract traded on the Singapore International Monetary Exchange (Simex) and Osaka Securities Exchange, ostensibly through what was, at least initially, a low-risk arbitrage strategy that turned into a punt that the Nikkei index, which measures the performance of 225 blue-chip Japanese companies, would not fall. It did.

The large positions held by Barings had not gone unnoticed. The London office had been queried by Simex. An internal audit in August 1994 emphasised the 'excessive concentration of responsibilities' in the Singapore office's chief trader and general manager. As early as March 1992 a letter from the managing director of Barings Futures in Singapore to the head of the bank's equity broking and trading group in London expressed concern about reporting lines, saying: '. . . once again we are in danger of setting up a structure which will subsequently prove to be disastrous and with which we will succeed in losing either a lot of money or client goodwill or probably both'. But Barings Futures (Singapore) contributed substantially to the bank's profits. London appears to have been reluctant to rein in an aggressive and seemingly successful trader.

Futures contracts are plain-vanilla products, not bafflingly complex derivatives structures, and they have been traded for years on regulated exchanges. Regulators' and practitioners' deepest fears about derivatives focus on over-the-counter trading of exotic products yet Barings was brought down not by the complexities of derivatives but by huge exposures in arguably the most straightforward of markets. Ultimately, what brought the situation to a head was the exchanges' system of margin calls.

The exchanges' margining systems are a crucial safety valve in futures trading. These, and capital-based position limits, are part of an exchange's armoury against dangerously large exposures. The Sydney Futures Exchange is not shy about calling senior management of a company to verify an unusually large exposure. According to the SFE's chief executive, Les Hosking, such a call has on at least one occasion led to a large position being unwound.

No market, bank or company can afford to be complacent regarding risk management. Commented Alan Greenspan, chairman of the US Federal Reserve, in the wake of Barings' collapse: 'Human nature is going to do what human nature has always done—bad things on occasion. Our job is to prevent that from becoming systemic.'

After a week of uncertainty about the fate of Barings, but amid continuing efforts to determine where blame for the losses should be sheeted, the giant Dutch-based international banking and insurance group, ING, took control of the centuries-old institution.

Derivatives were invented to help manage risk but they are not themselves risk-free. Nor do they eliminate risk; rather, derivatives enable market operators to transfer risk from a party who cannot, or does not want to, manage the risk adequately to one who can. Poorly managed, derivatives can increase risks for corporate users and professional dealers. Derivatives then get the blame when in fact the losses incurred are generally found to spring not from derivatives themselves but from a combination of inadequate management controls and insufficient supervision of treasury dealing activities, systems which are not adequate to capture and monitor the transactions and, in many cases, ignorance of all the ramifications of the strategy used. A further factor is a degree of greed that encourages companies to take a bet on the direction of interest rates, commodity prices, share prices or exchange rates.

The risks associated with derivatives are similar to those met in other trading and lending activities. A benefit of derivatives is that they enable price risks to be unbundled and re-packaged and so managed better than would otherwise be possible. This management does demand a greater-than-average degree of sophistication and vigilance on the part of dealers and end-users.

The risks chiefly associated with over-the-counter derivatives include:

- counterparty credit risk;
- market or price risk;
- market liquidity risk;

- valuation risk;
- operational risk;
- settlement risk;
- legal and regulatory risk;
- sovereign risk; and
- systemic (interconnecting) risk.

Counterparty credit risk

This arises from the possibility that a counterparty to a deal could default. Counterparty credit risk in futures markets rests with the exchange's clearing house and so is not a matter of concern for market participants. Over-the-counter derivatives traders, though, have no such protection—they have to assess the creditworthiness of every counterparty with which they deal. And, particularly when trading involves longer-term contracts, they have to monitor the credit-quality of counterparties, to be alert to any deterioration. A counterparty's credit status can change significantly within the five or ten-year time-frame of a derivative contract. The move to disclose an increasing amount of details about derivatives activities, evident in several banks' 1994 annual reports, helps round out the picture of an entity's exposures through derivatives. An absence of detail, on the other hand, feeds concerns about the possible 'domino' effect should a problem arise. The push continues for increasing, meaningful disclosure.

An important feature of derivatives, and one that is frequently cited in their support, is that failure by a counterparty to, say, a swap does not result in a loss anywhere near the gross amount involved. Swaps do not oblige counterparties to exchange gross cashflows but to deal in regular net payments. So the gross exposure to derivatives, as reported in company accounts, does not reflect a bank or company's exposure to loss.

The credit risk of a current exposure is limited to whatever it might cost one party to find a replacement, ie, to the price difference between the cost of the original transaction with the counterparty which has since failed to honour its obligations and the transaction with a new counterparty. A party forced to find cover for a large exposure, following counterparty failure, could strike liquidity problems which could add to costs. Credit risk also involves potential exposure and so calls for users to assess 'worst-case' scenarios and constantly ask themselves: 'What if?'

Generally, users and sellers of derivatives deal with top credit-rated counterparties to minimise potential credit risk.

There is considerable concern that, with the increase in credit risk assumed by dealers in derivatives, counterparty defaults could lead to widespread losses that could potentially spark a systemic crisis. The Group of Thirty did not subscribe to this view. Given that the rate of credit losses on derivatives has been lower than that produced by traditional banking activities, the group said that this 'indicates that by entering into derivatives transactions bank dealers have increased the average credit quality and diversity of risks to which they are exposed'. Credit risk is further reduced as players increasingly use bilateral, multi-product master agreements incorporating payment netting and close-out netting provisions. The US Federal Reserve has estimated that using such agreements cuts credit exposures by 40–60 per cent.

Market or price risk

Market or price risk is the possibility of loss because prices (interest rates, share prices and exchange rates) have shifted. Derivatives are very sensitive to changes in the value of the underlying financial instrument or commodity and so have to be constantly monitored.

Concerns about price or market risk relate mostly to:

- change in the price of the derivative which usually follows a change in the price of the underlying physical instrument or commodity or index;
- basis risk—the risk that a pair of prices or indexes might change in relative values, eg, the price differential between share-price index futures and physical share prices widens or narrows;
- spread risk—the risk of changes to the relative prices of similar instruments, eg, the margin between semi-government and commonwealth bonds; and

- yield curve risk—the risk of changes to the shape of the yield curve. This is particularly relevant when using instruments of different maturities to hedge.

Traders can manage the risks associated with derivatives by hedging their positions, eg, by taking an opposite but not exactly matched position in the same type of instrument with another counterparty and managing the residual risk, taking an opposite position and using a different instrument, taking an opposite position in the futures market which reduces overall risk or taking an offsetting position in a physical instrument with similar characteristics.

Market liquidity risk

Liquidity can be likened to a banker and credit—there when least needed and hard to find when most wanted. Liquidity risk is generally associated with the possibility that a large transaction in a given instrument could have considerable impact on its market price. In most financial markets, and Australia is no exception, derivatives trading tends to be concentrated among a group of major players so that there is concern that liquidity problems could arise if a large position had to be suddenly unwound. As a general rule, the more exotic the instrument, or the longer-term the transaction, the less liquid will be its market. Liquidity is more of a problem in over-the-counter markets, where operators face having to find a suitable offsetting counterparty for a customised product, than is the case with exchange-traded markets where standardised instruments are traded.

Valuation risk

Derivatives portfolios are marked to market to determine what the derivatives are currently worth and how much they might have changed because of a change in the value of the underlying instrument or asset. That says how much value is in the hedge. However, if an instrument has not been actively traded, so that its market value is not clear, there is an element of judgment in determining what is 'market'. Valuation risk concerns the possibility that a profit or loss on a transaction might not be correctly stated. Dealers might be keen to recognise profits straight away, whereas cautious employers might prefer to recognise only a portion of the profit and in the meantime set aside reserves for credit risk and any losses that might arise from unpredictable market movements.

Concerning market valuation methods, the Group of Thirty recommended:

> Derivatives portfolios of dealers should be valued based on mid-market levels less specific adjustments, or on appropriate bid or offer levels. Mid-market valuation adjustments should allow for expected future costs such as unearned credit spread, close-out costs, investing and funding costs, and administrative costs.

Valuation of derivatives is even more of a challenge when it involves long-term and exotic instruments. Derivatives are initially priced and subsequently valued using mathematical models that have no choice but to rely on an estimate of the likely volatility in the underlying instrument or asset over the term of the contract. Volatility may increase or decrease profits, depending on a company's position. Most derivatives trading firms have an internal independent unit checking traders' valuations of their derivatives. The firm's accountants would also keep an eye on these assumptions. Both the inputs to the models and the models themselves should be independently tested.

Operational risk

This type of risk arises from the possibility that management systems and controls are inadequate or that human error may occur. Such risk is present in other areas of the financial markets and in business generally but the demands and complexities of derivatives give it added importance. It is impossible to eradicate human error totally but, in any event, the biggest losses associated with derivatives have been attributed more to inadequate supervision and control (see case studies below and chapter 10).

Settlement risk

Financial transactions are rarely settled simultaneously, particularly when the parties to the transactions are in different time-zones, so that value is given by one before value is received by the other. Settlement risk centres on the possibility that a counterparty might default on settlement (payment and delivery of securities) or that something could go wrong in the settlement process.

However, while over-the-counter derivatives contracts involve large principal amounts, they give rise to small cashflows, so they represent minimal settlement risk. Daily global cashflows by, say, interest-rate swaps are dwarfed by daily settlements in foreign exchange. And the netting provisions of master agreements further reduce the flows, with counterparties making net payments rather than exchanging gross amounts.

Legal and regulatory risk

The Group of Thirty defines legal risk as the risk of loss because a contract cannot be enforced. Legal risk can relate to uncertainties regarding the status of a new instrument, eg, is it a security or a futures contract? Or it can involve concerns about a counterparty's capacity to deal and so the enforceability of a contract. To minimise uncertainties it is vital that documentation should clearly set out all the risks, rights and obligations. Also, market participants must keep a close watch on developments to ensure that any regulatory change enacted does not adversely affect the ability of counterparties to meet their obligations.

The Group of Thirty recommended that legislators, regulators and supervisors, including central banks, work in concert with dealers and end-users to identify and remove any remaining legal and regulatory uncertainties with respect to:

- the form of documentation required to create legally enforceable agreements (statute of frauds);
- the capacity of parties, such as government entities, insurance companies, pension funds and building societies, to enter into transactions (*ultra vires*);
- the enforceability of bilateral close-out netting and collateral arrangements in bankruptcy;
- the enforceability of multi-branch netting arrangements in bankruptcy; and
- the legality/enforceability of derivatives transactions.

Sovereign risk

This arises in cross-border interest-rate swaps and in currency swaps and concerns a country's financial status, possibly also its political stability, and certainly its ability to meet financial obligations. Sovereign risk arises not only if a country's financial integrity is in question but also if its government changes the rules, say, by introducing foreign-exchange controls which inhibit the free flow of capital and so repayments to a foreign investor.

Systemic risk

Systemic risk—the risk that one institution or market sector will get into difficulties which will spread to others, causing widespread problems for many, even the global financial system—gives regulators nightmares. The Group of Thirty identified three elements in derivatives trading which differentiate them from traditional activities: transparency, legal risk and market linkage. Transparency and legal risk are possible sources of systemic risk, as are credit and settlement risk. While there is no consensus on which aspects of derivatives trading give rise to systemic concerns, possible sources also include:

Size and complexity: Although the face values of derivatives involve staggering volumes of money, the amounts at risk in derivative contracts are quite moderate compared with the exposures sustained through lending, bond-trading and foreign exchange. The value of global derivatives positions is estimated to be a mere 2 or 3 per cent of the principal amounts and even that exaggerates the picture because it takes no account of netting. So sheer size is not the chief source of worry. As to complexity, the Group of Thirty emphasised several times in its report that the risks involved with derivatives are the same as those managed in conventional financial markets activities: credit risk, market risk, legal risk and operational risk. The complexity of derivatives, if they are properly managed, is not their major threat. However, it is the complexity of derivatives that is at the source of legal and operational risk, and to a lesser extent credit and market risk.

Concentration: Derivatives trading tends to be concentrated in large volumes among fairly few hands. The top eight banks in the US accounted for 86 per cent of over-the-counter interest-rate derivatives and 88 per cent of over-the-counter currency derivatives at the end of 1991. As Table 9.1 shows, the top five banks in Australia accounted for 80 per cent of currency options and 70 per cent of interest-rate swaps.

While major players do account for a large share of trading, the number of derivatives players is increasing. ISDA (International Swaps and Derivatives Association) membership totalled 150 by late 1993, treble the number of primary dealers in US government bonds and more than six times the number of active market-makers in Australian commonwealth government bonds.

Lack of transparency: Transparency is relevant at three levels: within a company, when reporting to creditors and shareholders, and in industry information.

Internally, the risks associated with derivatives are becomingly increasingly clear to management following widespread use of practices such as dealers using marking-to-market as a risk-management technique. Greater transparency would be useful in public reporting; however, the trading income produced by derivatives can fluctuate wildly with a correspondingly erratic effect on a bank's share price. A discussion paper, *Public Disclosure of Market and Credit Risks by Financial Intermediaries*, prepared by a Bank for International Settlements working group chaired by Peter Fisher of the Federal Reserve Bank of New York, contained a recommendation regarding market risk disclosure and credit risk disclosure:

> All financial intermediaries, regulated and unregulated, should move in the direction of publicly disclosing periodic quantitative information which expresses, in summary form, the estimates relied upon by firm management of:
>
> - the market risks in the relevant portfolio or portfolios, as well as the firm's actual performance in managing the market risks in these portfolios;
> - the counterparty credit risks arising from its trading and risk-management activities, including current credit exposures, potential future credit exposure, and counterparty

Table 9.1   Concentration of derivatives activity

	Top 5 %	Top 10 %
FX forward	80	92
Currency swaps	66	84
Currency options	80	98
Interest-rate swaps	71	87
Interest-rate futures	83	98
Interest-rate options	83	96
Gold contracts	100	100
Total	76	91

Source: Supervising Banks' Derivative Activities, Brian Gray, chief manager, policy development and research, bank supervision department, Reserve Bank of Australia, March 1994.

creditworthiness, in a form which permits evaluation of the firm's performance in managing these credit risks.

Illiquidity: There is concern that, given their complexity, portfolios of derivatives could be hard to sell or transfer. However, experience has shown otherwise, with derivatives easily lending themselves to being closed out or transferred. The ability to 'unbundle' a derivative, ie, separate it into different components each of which is quite liquid, is an advantage. However, a crisis can have the effect of turning a previously liquid derivative into an illiquid one. An old market saying is that anything can always be sold, but at a price. For example, during a crisis such as the collapse of the European Monetary System in 1992 the market continues to trade but with dramatically widening spreads so that closing out transactions becomes very expensive. Dealers use stress-testing to assess the possible impact of illiquidity on their portfolios.

Unregulated entities: The major dealers in derivatives are the large banks and securities firms which are regulated and supervised. However, there is always the risk that a new entity will creep through the supervisory/regulatory net. Market operators select as counterparties only the top credits—especially if dealing with an unregulated entity—because only the top credits have substantial limits and so can be major players. Derivatives dealers use their own credit judgment rather than relying on the regulatory status of a counterparty.

Market linkages: Derivatives, aided by communications technology, have undeniably linked financial markets around the world to an unprecedented degree. This can be seen as a source of strength or a potential weakness. Those such as the Group of Thirty see the linkage as a strength because derivatives can be used to distribute volatility from one sector into the wider community. Thus any financial shocks that occur are absorbed by a greater number of participants rather than one sector alone. However, it can also be argued that through derivatives a shock can be transmitted more rapidly than before. According to the Group of Thirty, 'academic research indicates that derivatives trading does not increase volatility in underlying markets'.

Legal risks: The Group of Thirty study states that legal risks 'remain significant and have the potential to create systemic problems'. Being very new, over-the-counter derivatives are not always easily covered by existing legal provisions. G30 concluded: 'While it is hard to find justification for the view that derivatives pose a greater systemic threat than other financial activities, there is no room for complacency.'

The growing complexity of derivatives, the concentration of activity among a select group, the liquidity of the products and the linkages among world markets are well known and controllable elements of derivatives trading. What is not controllable is the motive of the dealers and users—and the dangerous elements here are greed, over-confidence and a determination to squeeze the last drop of value out of a deal.

The following case studies are examples of organisations that tripped; mostly, the problems can be tracked back to leverage and/or inadequate supervision and control.

METALLGESELLSCHAFT AG

Metallgesellschaft Corporation (MG), the US subsidiary of the giant German metals, mining and industrial group Metallgesellschaft AG, lost some $US1.8 billion ($A2.5 billion) through an ill-thought-out strategy involving oil futures and options. Much has been written about MG's strategy, where it went wrong and whether ultimately its board panicked over what came down to a severe liquidity problem and crystallised paper losses into real ones. The episode sparked a rush of academic articles contradicting the popular line that MG had indulged in a risky hedging strategy. One paper, by Professor Franklin Edwards of Columbia University, stated: 'MG's hedging strategy went wrong because of misleading hedge accounting and disclosure principles, funding rigidities and lack of understanding at the level of the MG supervisory board (board of directors).' Leaving aside the academic arguments over MG's strategy, who was to blame and whether the situation could have been better handled, it seems inescapable that a serious flaw in MG's strategy was the basis risk between the long-term contracts it was hedging and the short-term futures and over-the-counter contracts it entered into as a hedge. This left MG covering market or price risk but left it exposed to basis risk. And this created a fresh risk: liquidity. The company was left with a cashflow crisis.

MG's strategy

Through its subsidiary, MG Refining and Marketing, MG sold an enormous amount of five-to-ten-year heating oil and gasoline fixed-price supply contracts to customers at prices ranging between six to eight cents above spot. (A relevant point is the difficulty of finding a suitable hedging strategy for such long-term fixed-price supply contracts.) Business boomed. MG now had an exposure to the price at which it would be able to obtain oil to supply these customers. So the company hedged these contracts with over-the-counter swaps and oil futures contracts on Nymex. That removed MG's price risk should oil prices rise, but, as events were to show, it created new hazards: liquidity risk (from having to meet margin calls on futures contracts) and basis risk because MG was using short-term contracts as a hedge which had to be rolled over at new premiums/discounts, and rolling over short-term contracts did not necessarily provide the required oil price ten years hence.

Reflecting its growing business, MG's position in Nymex became huge, more than twice the exchange's usual 24 000-contract limit, because MG, like other distributors of oil products, had secured an exemption from the hedging limit. Its futures position, combined with its over-the-counter contracts, was estimated to give MG commitments equal to 160 million barrels of oil a day—or more than 80 times the daily output of Kuwait.

MG's strategy was based on an assumption that the oil market would remain in backwardation (forward prices lower than spot) enabling MG to roll over the contracts at a profit. But the oil market moved into contango (forward prices higher than spot) and, as spot oil prices fell in late 1993, MG was increasingly squeezed, losing money rolling over its futures positions while cash inflow from supply agreements fell well behind the demand for margin calls and payments on over-the-counter contracts. The company was developing a horrendous funding mismatch as the spread widened between long-term and short-term oil prices. As increasing collateral against huge and deteriorating futures positions was demanded, the company simply ran out of cash and credit lines. MG had to borrow from its parent.

The hedging strategy nearly bankrupted Metallgesellschaft. The parent company stated in its 1993 annual report that its North American subsidiary 'generated losses which are threatening the Metallgesellschaft Group's existence. Metall Corp has tried to hedge long-term delivery commitments towards customers who had concluded fixed-price contracts with short-term revolving futures dealings'. It would appear that MG's reporting and management systems did not keep adequate track of the company's exposures and risks; the strategy was implemented over a couple of years and the full picture not revealed to MG's board until December 1993.

MG began unwinding its web of futures and OTC positions at a time when the oil price had hit a five-year low, turning paper losses into real ones. Early in 1994 oil prices rose, prompting comment that MG would have done better to sit tight, but the amounts needed to cover margin calls apparently ruled out that alternative. The liquidation was executed progressively in an attempt not to further undermine already depressed prices. The crisis was over, at the cost of many millions of dollars and several heads at MG and its parent company.

A major paper on MG's problems, by Nobel Prize-winning

economist Merton Miller and academic Christopher Culp, asserts that MG's problems arose from the large funding requirements of a forward portfolio hedged with futures when the market moves against the futures leg. As one energy derivatives expert told *Risk* magazine:

> Because these funding requirements became large enough to strain MG's credit relationships with its counterparties and banks, it forced MG into a 'gambler's ruin' scenario—that is, a forced withdrawal from the table because its chips ran out before it could play out the game with what would have been a winning hand.

The MG case clearly demonstrates how, when undertaking a hedging transaction to eliminate one risk, a company substitutes a new set of risks that have to be monitored and managed.

PROCTER & GAMBLE, GIBSON GREETINGS INC AND MEAD CORPORATION

According to an analysis by *Risk* magazine, the cases of Procter & Gamble, Gibson Greetings and Mead Corporation involved using swaps which were pegged to a complex formula that relied on each company expressing a strong view that interest rates would not rise. The formula was used to determine the spread to LIBOR that each company would pay, after the first reset period, for the remainder of the swap. Reported *Risk*:

> In particular, these companies were betting through this formula that rates would not rise on the five-year and 30-year points in the US Treasury curve and, in the case of P&G, on similar points on the German Treasury curve as well. In exchange, each company was potentially left with floating-rate debt at LIBOR minus 75–150 basis points if the formula worked in its favour (ie, if rates remained unchanged or fell).

However, the companies were vulnerable if rates rose, which they did.

Procter & Gamble, one of the world's leading consumer goods companies and a seasoned user of derivatives, entered into $US and deutschmark leveraged interest-rate swap transactions which, put simply, enabled it to take a big punt on interest-rate movements. The rise in interest rates left P&G's bet on the wrong side and the company lost $US157 million. In a press release accompanying its March 1994 third-quarter report, when the company announced the $US157 million pre-tax loss stemming from closing out two leverage swaps, it said the decision to close out followed a sharp rise in interest rates:

> Procter & Gamble, like many large corporations, has successfully used interest-rate swaps to manage exposure to interest and exchange rates, and to reduce the cost of borrowings. Unlike the other swaps the company has historically used, it turned out that the two leveraged swaps in question were based on highly complex formulas that multiplied the effect of interest rates increasing. These types of transactions are inconsistent with the company's policy.

However, according to industry sources, P&G had a reputation as an aggressive hedger.

The leverage formula is understood to have generated interest-rate exposures for P&G to the tune of some 100 times face value—ie, swaps with a face value of $100 million would generate exposure to the market of $10 billion. The leverage was such that every one basis-point movement in the market cost P&G 100 basis points on the notional face value of the transaction. The leverage involved in the swap was twofold:

- the formula included an explicit leverage multiple; and
- the interest rate for the rest of life of the swap was established at the end of year one and locked in for the remainder of the swap, so that a loss at the end of the first year was also incurred for the life of the swap.

Details were slow to emerge but it appears the formula ran like this: put in $1 today and in one year's time you get back $1 plus 20 times the interest rate determined at the outset, less the rate prevailing one year hence. So if the rate at the outset is, say, 6 per cent, but the rate in one year's time is expected to be 5 per cent, at the end of year one you would expect/hope to receive the original $1 plus 20 times 6 per cent less 5 per cent = 20 times 1 per cent = 20 per cent of your principal so you would receive $1.20. The formula held considerable appeal while interest rates were expected to fall. However, if interest rates rise, substitute 8 per cent for the 5 per cent and the sum is –2 per cent x 20 = –40 per cent, so instead of receiving $1.20 you get 60 cents. But under the swap you have to pay $1, ie lose 40 cents. Moreover, this loss of 40 per cent of the principal at the end of that first year is lost for every year of the swap. On a principal of $100 million that turns into a loss of $160 million over a four-year swap. With such leverage, much is made if all goes well, much is lost if not.

P&G chairman Edwin Artzt commented after P&G's announcement of the loss: 'Derivatives like these are dangerous and we were badly burned.' But derivatives are not in themselves dangerous—the dangers lie in how they are used. They are merely tools which can be put to good or bad use. The US comptroller of the currency said in an address in April 1994 that 'according to analysts, Procter & Gamble made a low-probability, high-risk bet that interest rates would fall . . .'

Addressing a conference in Sydney in 1994, Stephen Wood, of Macquarie Bank Risk Advisory Services Limited, said that P&G 'had volume and delta sensitivities to market movements so that the impact of future market movements on the company's swaps was greatly amplified'.

P&G took legal action against Bankers Trust New York, the bank which had designed and sold it the swaps, alleging deceptive sales technique.

Gibson Greetings followed its announcement of a $3 million loss on leveraged swaps with a charge of $16.7 million against earnings in April 1994, also due to swaps. Like P&G, Gibson did not disclose much detail about the transactions. Gibson sued Bankers Trust New York, claiming the bank had failed to disclose the risks of the derivatives it had sold. The suit was settled out of court. Another US company, paper manufacturer Mead Corporation, lost $US7.4 million from hedging transactions including a leveraged interest-rate swap.

The swaps structures were unusually aggressive for use by a company, prompting comment that they smacked more of trading than hedging. Overall, leveraged swaps of the kind used by P&G, Gibson Greetings and Mead are a very small proportion of the trillions of dollars in global notional swap principals.

HAMMERSMITH & FULHAM

The case involving the London borough of Hammersmith & Fulham raised quite different issues from those cited above but, as the first serious hiccup in the swaps market, it is a landmark in the history of derivatives. And it sent shivers of apprehension through financial communities around the world.

The case centred on the close-to-600 swap transactions involving a notional £6.2 billion executed between 1987 and 1989 by the London borough whose annual revenues at that time totalled £85 million. Hammersmith & Fulham was more than hedging, it was punting on interest rates—and it lost. In 1988 the district auditor warned the council that it could be acting outside its authority in the swaps market and the council responded by curtailing its activities. Its auditor initiated proceedings by trying to have the deals declared invalid, saying they were outside the scope of a local borough. In November 1989 the court held that the council was not empowered to enter into capital market transactions and that its entry into such transactions with a view to profit was unreasonable and unlawful. The court was alarmed that not only was a local council trying to make a profit from trading in the capital markets but that many of its transactions were highly speculative and involved sizeable financial risk.

The judgment was bad news for the more than 50 banks which had entered into similar transactions with some 70 local authorities—transactions that had now been deemed illegal. The councils were therefore not liable for payments under those contracts on which they would otherwise have suffered large losses. That left the banks with potentially hundreds of millions of dollars at risk. The banks appealed against the decision and in February 1990 the court of appeal in part allowed their plea, saying that a local authority, as part of its duty to manage borrowings and investments prudently, could enter into interest-rate swap transactions provided they were to manage risk and not to trade. Later that year, the House of Lords upheld the original view of the courts, ie, that a local council was not empowered to enter into capital markets transactions and so the swaps, being outside the council's authority, were not binding on it. The House of Lords ruled finally in April 1991 that all swap market transactions entered into by a London council were illegal. This left some 80 banks owed around £500–600 million by 131 local councils. Banks were left to seek compensation through the courts individually.

The case raised awareness around the world of the need to be certain about a counterparty's legal capacity to enter into a swap transaction. Legal firms everywhere benefited as nervous banks called for advice regarding the enforceability of contracts. In Australia there are entities whose capacity to contract is not clear, eg, building societies, which must only use derivatives as a hedge, raising the concern of defining categorically what is a hedge and what is speculation. Problems also arise in the case of fund managers where it is not always clear which trust they are dealing for, nor is it clear where the counterparty to a swap with a fund manager ranks should there be cause to determine who has first claim on the assets of the trust.

ORANGE COUNTY

In December 1994 California's Orange County delivered a blow to financial markets confidence when the municipality filed for bankruptcy protection, recording the largest municipal crash in US history. Orange County's $US7.4 billion ($A9.6 billion) investment fund announced it faced losses of some $US2 billion following a combination of a steep rise in interest rates and a highly leveraged investment strategy. Irrespective of the complexities of its transactions, Orange County's problem was simple: it wound up being caught in the archetypal squeeze, paying more for its borrowings than it was earning on investments.

It appears that Orange County had for some years adopted an aggressive investment strategy that relied on using complex instruments such as inverse floaters (notes whose interest rate is structured as a fixed rate less a floating index, so that the interest rate on the notes rises or falls in the reverse direction to the general direction of interest rates) and a high degree of leverage facilitated by several billion dollars worth of fixed-term repurchase agreements (repos, see chapter 8). Structured securities such as inverse floaters are not regarded as derivatives* but they enable a similar degree of leverage and they enable an investor to take a position (punt) on the direction of interest rates. Orange County's strategy was based on a view—essentially a bet—that interest rates would continue to fall in 1994, an approach that caught out many that year as rates in fact climbed. Orange County filed for bankruptcy protection after one of the several Wall Street firms with which it had written fixed-term repos decided to sell the securities it held because the municipality had missed a $200 million payment due to the firm under the $2.6 billion repo arrangement. By filing for bankruptcy protection, Orange County hoped to prevent the other firms from doing the same. However, legal opinion was that the bankruptcy regulations do not apply to repos.

*The Group of Thirty said of structured securities such as inverse/reverse floaters:

> Many structured securities exhibit risk/return characteristics similar to global derivatives. Most are sold to sophisticated institutional investors capable of analysing their risk/return, leverage and liquidity characteristics . . . It is important, however, that institutional investors understand and manage the risks of the securities they are purchasing . . . the complexity of owning and managing structured securities can and should be addressed through an understanding of derivatives transactions and their risks.

CHAPTER 10

MANAGING THE RISKS

The scare stories about derivatives have prompted a concentrated focus on management and controls to prevent losses. Most losses that have involved derivatives have arisen from situations where common sense was ignored in favour of aggressive leverage and where management, because of inadequate procedures or technical systems, lack of information or ignorance, did not appear to be fully aware of the ramifications of the transactions. Derivatives are demanding. Everyone involved should understand the nature of the transactions and systems should be adequate to monitor and manage the risk. There is nothing mysterious or impossibly hard to grasp with derivatives. But those not on the coalface tend to allow themselves to be baffled by the numbers and the jargon, or to use the 'complexity' of the deal as an excuse for not understanding the risks involved. No board member or senior manager can afford that approach.

Senior managers are under a duty of care to be technically knowledgeable in areas for which they hold responsibility. If, as tends to happen, new products are developed in which they have no hands-on experience, they have to ensure that at least they understand how they operate. For their part, dealers in derivatives should have a clear understanding of why a particular client wants to use a particular derivatives product, just as a lending officer would want to be satisfied with a borrower's reasons and capacity to borrow.

What is also important is a grasp of the different challenges facing, say, a bank as against a corporate when using derivatives, and the different levels of understanding demanded by a corporate board member, a bank board member, a chief executive, a treasury head and a dealer.

Managing risk is not new for banks and investment banks—these institutions have been in the business of taking and managing risks for centuries. Derivatives create an extension of that basic risk-taking; they do not involve unfamiliar risks. What is different is that derivatives trading demands a new dimension of technological support to ensure the associated risks are adequately measured, monitored and managed. The worry is that the very interdependence of the risks created by derivatives makes them hard to track and cover.

Corporates face a harder challenge. Managing financial risk is not part of their core business, as it is for banks, and a company whose main function is turning out, say, washing machines has to think long and hard about what resources, funds and staff it wants to devote to an in-house treasury which might contribute only a minuscule proportion of its profits. Moreover, the board of a company making washing machines might well represent an excellent pool of talent but a grasp of derivatives might not have been a requirement when each was appointed. Corporates deciding against the establishment of a large in-house treasury—as is usually the case—would leave the technicalities of using derivatives to their banks or investment banks.

Company policy regarding the use of derivatives would still, however, be set by the board, possibly in consultation with the company's risk-management committee, so it is essential that board members understand what is involved. That means they must know enough to be able to ask relevant questions and understand the answers. If a board presentation has not been understood it should be repeated until it is. If a treasury staffer cannot clearly explain a derivative transaction to the board then it is questionable whether he or she understands it. And staff are exposed if the board is in the dark.

It is the role of the board and management to decide:

- how much of a company's exposure to hedge and how much in the way of risks it should undertake;

- who within the company can inititate a derivatives transaction and up to what limit;
- the type of counterparty with which the company can deal; and
- up to what level of exposure.

The Group of Thirty said about senior management:

> Dealers and end-users should use derivatives in a manner consistent with the overall risk-management and capital policies approved by their boards of directors. These policies should be reviewed as business and market circumstances change. Policies governing derivatives use should be clearly defined, including the purposes for which these transactions are to be undertaken. Senior management should approve procedures and controls to implement these policies, and management at all levels should enforce them.

Given that derivatives risk-management is still evolving, senior management should regularly re-evaluate the company's appetite for risk and risk-management procedures.

Within treasury, whether in a bank or a corporate treasury, it is essential that the people trading the instruments understand them and their impact, that systems capture their characteristics, that reporting procedures are properly measuring changes in a portfolio of derivatives, and that duties within treasury are properly defined. That requires a segregation of four functions: those who initiate a deal (dealing function), those who make the payments (confirmation and settlement), those who revalue the portfolio (back/middle office) and those who approve deals and set limits (credit function). Strict reporting guidelines would include daily reports to the treasury head, a weekly report to a general manager, a detailed monthly report to the board and possibly another monthly report to a general manager or chief executive. The objective is to ensure everyone is aware of activity in derivatives, what the exposures are and how they are being handled. Treasury presentations to the board, in a bank and in a company, are an important part of the process of keeping the board not just informed but educated. To be meaningful, reports to the board and senior management must be fully detailed. Finally, adequate audit procedures underpin all the above.

Such has been the emphasis on the need to upgrade risk-management systems when trading derivatives that by the time the Group of Thirty reported in 1993 most derivatives traders had taken to steps to:

- value their positions daily by marking them to market;
- establish an independent risk-management unit within the trading division;
- recognise the importance of monitoring potential counterparty exposures that might result from future market movements as well as measuring existing exposures (through marking to market);
- take into account possible changes in credit and administration costs that could affect longer-term transactions;
- integrate front and back-office systems to minimise reporting errors;
- upgrade technology to cope with the complexities of derivatives;
- ensure senior management were keeping pace with developments in the trading room; and
- standardise documentation for derivatives activities.

BACK OFFICE

Derivatives trading has brought fresh challenges for the back office. The back office's role in derivatives trading is to record, document and confirm transactions just as it does for other securities activities. This is a vital element in preventing instances of dealer fraud, such as dealing at off-market rates or mis-stating the volatilities used in revaluing an options portfolio. There is justification for the view that the rapid development of derivatives and the increasing complexity of the transactions demand special skills and accuracy in procedures and systems. The back office must be supported by controls that cover all aspects of a transaction, from the moment it is dealt to settlement and administration, accounting, reporting and review. Back office and front office (dealing, marketing, hedging) must each understand what the other is doing. Derivatives have not brought new risk factors but they present a combination of risks, in the form of new products, that demand systems with unpar-alleled flexibility. For example, swaps and options combined to create swaptions, spreads and options to create spreadtions, and such transactions have to be separated—*unbundled*, in traders' language—to be processed and properly managed for risk.

It is vital that any error is discovered as soon as possible, particularly in the case of long-term forward transactions where, say, several months or even a year might intervene between trade and settlement dates with no cashflow or margining involved. The confirmation process, where the back office receives written acknowledgement of a deal, should detect mistakes.

The Group of Thirty highlighted four areas—people, systems, authority and risk management—requiring attention to ensure that the back office is abreast of innovations in the front office and has in place sufficient controls to cope with these. No-one in the high-speed, pressurised and volatile world of derivatives trading wants to be surprised.

People

It is generally accepted that back office staff handling derivatives transactions need higher skills than their counterparts coping with the more 'conventional' financial markets activities. Just as derivatives trading has bred new specialist dealers, so the back office demands specialist staff who understand the structured transactions traded, can identify the various associated risks and process the transactions properly. It is vital that those processing, confirming, controlling and settling derivatives transactions understand the business; it is equally important that those responsible for risk-management and internal audits have a clear grasp of the issues and risks involved. Back-office staff must have sufficient status within an institution to be able to query or challenge a trader's action. Many cases of fraud have involved a 'star' who has earned profits of such dimensions that no-one has dared to question his or her decisions.

Systems

The Group of Thirty recommended:

Dealers and end-users must ensure that adequate systems for data capture, processing, settlement and management reporting are in place so that derivatives transactions are conducted in an orderly and efficient manner in compliance with management policies. Dealers should have risk-management systems that measure the risks incurred in their derivatives activities including market and credit risks. End-users should have risk-management systems that measure the risks incurred in their derivatives activities based upon their nature, size and complexity.

Powerful technical systems are essential to capture information, process and settle trades, and carry out management reporting. Systems have to be able to unbundle transactions into different risks and deal with them appropriately. Derivatives require stringent controls because:

- they offer opportunities for leverage that can create large underlying positions;
- price and liquidity can be volatile;
- they are a specialised market that has spawned its own language and its own breed of professional traders who transact complex deals at high speed and in large volumes, confronting management and boards with new challenges in terms of monitoring compliance;
- there is a risk of default by a counterparty;
- the instruments are increasingly complex; and
- they can involve long-term positions which increase exposures to credit and price risk.

The major players in derivatives could not carry out their business without advanced technology. Most have their own research and technology teams developing pricing models and management information systems. But the demands can go beyond the resources of in-house teams so that a new software industry has developed to provide computer systems specifically designed for derivatives business. Such has been the pace of development and expansion in derivatives trading that the larger operators tend to use a variety of systems.

The size and scope of a system is determined by the size and scope of the derivatives business. The level of internal control over derivatives should match the nature and extent of the underlying risks. A major, active derivatives dealer requires far greater sophistication in systems than a corporate end-user with fewer transactions to manage. However, even such operators should have systems that can aggregate exposures and analyse the associated risk. An increase in derivatives business should be matched by increasing sophistication and integration in systems so that risks can be properly monitored and managed. The key for the big players is integrated systems—integrated across the different instruments so that risks can be assessed, and integrated between front and back office, and between the trading desk and those who monitor credit risk.

The major derivatives dealers have to make considerable investment in systems that integrate front and back offices and other management information systems. Effective systems are essential when assessing credit risk and market risk, and for ensuring that transactions are marked-to-market and for netting.

To be effective, a control system must promptly identify and report errors in accounting records, incorrectly recorded positions, inappropriate management decisions and unauthorised trading. A fundamental control in derivatives business, as in all other areas of financial markets trading, is the separation of dealing, settling and accounting areas.

Authority

The Group of Thirty observed that management of dealers and end-users should designate among the staff who is authorised to commit their institutions to derivatives transactions. This applies to end-users as much as to dealers. Ideally, the board should nominate those responsible for derivatives business and all levels of management must be clear about who can commit the company to a deal. It is the responsibility of management to ensure that trading is carried out by the appropriate staff.

Market risk and credit-risk management

The growth and increasing complexity of derivatives have thrown up huge challenges for control systems. Traders have to be constantly and fully aware of market risk, be in a position to evaluate that risk and ensure it is not just monitored but properly managed. Limits must be established so that the system can then produce daily reports comparing the company's positions and commitments with its limits. Limits are a vital element of credit risk-management, to ensure that unwanted credit exposures are not initiated. The limit discipline is imposed to contain the damage that could be caused by an unwelcome movement in the value of exposures; it follows, then, that the method used to recognise changes in the value of the positions must be accurate. The formulas used to value positions should be independently checked. Further, limits are not effective if they are not monitored independently, ie, by someone other than the dealers. Most dealing institutions carry out a daily management review of positions from a market-risk standpoint. Recommendation 5 of the G30 is that market risk is 'best measured as "value at risk" using probability analysis based upon a common confidence interval (eg, two standard deviations) and time horizon (eg, a one-day exposure)'. Using value-at-risk, a dealer can:

- evaluate potential losses and the likelihood of their occurring;
- adjust for changes in the volatility of financial markets;
- use a common denominator to show potential losses for different instruments and currencies; and
- aggregate risks of different portfolios for all maturities and markets.

The advantage of value-at-risk is that a dealer can reduce the complex elements of derivatives, such as delta, gamma and theta, to a single concept of value-at-risk or earnings-at-risk which is easily conveyed to, say, a board of directors. G30 comments:

> Reducing market risks across derivatives to a single common denominator makes aggregation, comparison and risk control easier. 'Value at risk' is the expected loss from an adverse market movement with a specified probability over a particular period of time . . . Value at risk should encompass changes in all major market risk components listed [in recommendation 5]. The difficulty in applying the technique of value at risk increases with the complexity of the risks being managed. For comparability, value at risk should be calculated to a common confidence interval and time horizon.

Best practice dictates that dealers should have an independent unit dedicated to measuring and monitoring market risk. End-users would tend to review positions monthly.

The legal, compliance and financial control departments provide additional controls. The internal audit is an important influence on procedures and controls. To be effective, the internal audit must be independent of management and have adequate resources including people who understand the business. Internal audits should be frequent; however, they are useless if those carrying them out do not know what they are doing. Internal audit staff must be trained so that they understand the products used in derivatives trading as well as the models used to price them.

Internal accounting practices contribute to risk management by:

- ensuring trading positions are marked to market;
- ensuring, where derivatives are used to hedge or manage risk, that gains or losses on the instrument are accounted for in the same way as gains or losses on the underlying position; and
- checking that amounts due to and from the same counterparty are offset only where effective netting arrangements are in place.

STRESS-TESTING

Stress-testing involves marking a portfolio to market and then analysing the impact on its value of large price movements. The objective is to see the effect on the portfolio of unfavourable shifts in interest rates and exchange rates. Stress-testing should be carried out before entering a transaction to determine what risks are involved, and repeated regularly once the transaction is under way.

The Group of Thirty recommended that dealers regularly perform simulations to determine how their portfolio would perform under stress conditions.

> Simulations of improbable market environments are important in risk analysis because many assumptions that are valid for normal markets may no longer hold true in abnormal markets. These

simulations should reflect both historical events and future possibilities. Stress scenarios should include not only abnormally large market swings but also periods of prolonged inactivity. The tests should consider the effect of price changes on the mid-market value of the portfolio, as well as changes in the assumptions about the adjustments to mid-market (such as the impact that decreased liquidity would have on close-out costs). Dealers should evaluate the results of stress tests and develop contingency plans accordingly.

To be effective, scenario stress-testing should include extreme situations, however imaginary or bizarre they might seem. Markets are regularly knocked off course by the unexpected and outlandish.

Stress-testing is one way of quantifying exposure to reductions in market liquidity. It is also recommended that dealers formulate a disaster plan to deal with worst-case situations. And risk-management procedures should be in place before a new product starts to trade, to ensure that as many eventualities as possible are covered.

CHAPTER 11

....

REGULATION AND LEGISLATION

The growth and inventiveness in derivatives activities has outrun the scope of Australia's Corporations Law, creating disturbing legal and commercial uncertainty. Combined with patchy understanding of how derivatives work, and a global nervousness about the risk implications of these new, and in some instances complex, products, this uncertainty has forced regulators and legislators not just in Australia but around the world back to the drawing board to bring the relevant legislation up to speed. The objective is to ensure investor protection and maintain the integrity of financial markets.

In carrying out this task the legislators have been able to draw on a plethora of studies, reports and surveys, such as the G30 report in 1993, a report released in the following year by the US Government Accounting Office, a Reserve Bank survey of Australian banks' activities in derivatives and a report on over-the-counter (OTC) derivatives released in May 1994 by the Australian Securities Commission (ASC).

The ASC recommended a thorough review of the law as it relates to derivatives markets. Its review focused on two themes: the implications of OTC derivatives market activity for investor protection, especially regarding retail participants, and measures that would contribute to the financial stability of derivatives providers and the overall integrity of the OTC derivatives markets. The Corporations Law, in force since 1991 and combining the earlier Securities Industry Act and Futures Industry Act, regulates securities (Chapter 7) and futures (Chapter 8). So derivatives are regulated through the Corporations Law if they fall within the definition of a security or of a futures contract. The law tries to fit all instruments into one category or the other; however, markets can construct them so that distinctions are blurred. Some derivatives are neither a security nor a futures contract, eg, an over-the-counter commodity option, and so are not captured by the law. This leaves scope for derivatives to be structured explicitly to fall outside the law.

Gaps in the law are an inevitable consequence of rapid market innovation. Over the years, though, the number of products falling into the gap has increased. And, in the view of some, there is a pressing commercial imperative to introduce a flexible interim regulatory solution to enable the development of new products.

Many transactions, such as interest-rate and currency swaps and forward-rate agreements (but not commodity and equity swaps), are specifically excluded from Chapter 8 if a bank or merchant bank is on one side. For those not confident that a transaction meets this exclusion, the ASC late in 1993 introduced its 'safe harbour' concept as an interim measure covering transactions carried out between sophisticated professionals.

A transaction either:

- qualifies for the specific money-market exclusion; or
- is a futures contract and traded on an exempt futures market (a market specifically relieved of most Chapter 8 regulations because both parties to the transaction are 'sophisticated', ie professional not retail operators); or
- is a futures contract and so conducting a market in futures would breach Chapter 8; or
- is structured so that it is not a futures contract, but it then risks being caught by the Gaming and Betting Acts of the different states (as a bet and so unenforceable).

What is traded over-the-counter potentially falls into Chapters 7 or 8, or between the two. The ASC's 1994 report on OTC derivatives addresses the regulatory structure, the gaps, safe-harbour concept, the exclusions and definitions of 'securities' and 'futures' with a view to producing a regulatory regime which caters for products on the basis of their function.

A major concern for the ASC is that a hapless retail investor—however that is defined—could come to grief in an increasingly complex world. Another concern is that professional markets have also been operating with a degree of legal uncertainty which is an inevitable accompaniment to new products. Markets tend to accept this—until a hiccup occurs, as in the landmark Hammersmith & Fulham case in London where the House of Lords ultimately held local boroughs did not have the power to enter into swaps transactions, a decision that created losses running into hundreds of millions for the banks involved.

THE REGULATORY FRAMEWORK IN AUSTRALIA

Australian law provides exhaustive definitions about what constitutes a futures contract and what a security. Section 72 of the Corporations Law describes four types of transactions that qualify as a futures contract:

- an eligible commodity agreement, eg, a contract covering something deliverable such as wool or bank bills;
- an adjustment agreement, being a contract based on an underlying item not capable of being delivered, eg, an index, and so is cash-settled, such as the SFE's share-price index (SPI) and bond futures contracts;
- a futures option, being options over eligible commodity agreements and adjustment agreements, such as an option over a SPI futures contract;
- an eligible exchange-traded option, being an option on a commodity or a specified index (not over a futures contract).

To fall within the definition of a 'futures contract' an agreement must be standardised. Specifically excluded from the definition of a 'futures contract' are currency and interest-rate swaps, and forward exchange-rate or forward interest-rate contracts involving an Australian bank or merchant bank. These exclusions, a hangover from a late amendment to the 1986 Futures Industry Bill, have drawn criticism because they create uncertainties.

Section 92 of the Corporations Law also identifies three categories of securities relevant to derivatives (the definition of 'securities' excludes futures contracts so a derivative cannot be both a futures contract and a security):

- an option as described in Chapter 7 of the Corporations Law;
- units of shares of a body corporate; and
- prescribed interests (which might include the rights under a futures contract or OTC derivatives not regulated by Chapter 8, depending on the arrangement struck between the provider of the derivative and the client).

Chapter 7 defines three types of options:

- an option giving a person a right to buy or sell securities at a specified price on or before a specified date (whether or not traded on an exchange);
- an option contract entered into on a securities exchange (or an exempt stockmarket, ie, a market relieved of most of the regulations of Chapter 7 because both parties to the transaction are sophisticated professionals) which confers a right to buy or sell an amount of a specified currency or a quantity of a specified commodity at a definite price;
- an option contract entered into on a securities exchange (or an exempt stockmarket) which confers a right to be paid an amount determined by comparing a specified number with a specified index.

The second and third types of option contracts would be eligible exchange-traded options if entered into on a futures exchange. Options over issued shares of a corporation will be within the first type.

THE REGULATORY REGIME

The approaches to regulation adopted by Chapter 7 and Chapter 8 of the Corporations Law apply many similar features to both securities and futures, including:

- licensing brokers and advisers;
- requiring licence holders to take responsibility for the actions of representatives;

- requiring clients' and brokers' funds to be separate and ensuring that brokers provide details of trading to clients;
- requiring a fund be established to compensate clients who have suffered loss through 'defalcation or fraudulent misuse of money' by a member of an exchange;
- providing a statutory framework to facilitate co-regulation of the industry by self-regulatory organisations and the ASC; and
- prohibiting certain forms of abusive behaviour.

However, there are two notable differences in approach. First, Chapter 7, covering securities, requires that disclosure in relation to the offer or issue of securities be made through a prospectus, whereas Chapter 8 requires futures brokers to give prospective clients information explaining the nature of futures contracts and the obligations and risks associated with trading in them.

Second, the regulation of futures, in common with regulatory regimes overseas, has as its basis the requirement of on-exchange trading, whereas no such requirement applies to transactions in securities. The ASC, in its report on OTC derivatives, comments on this point:

> In the US, the requirement that as a general rule futures
> contracts only be entered into on a designated 'contract market'
> has a lengthy legislative history. It was designed to regulate
> manipulative and deceptive practices and limit so-called
> 'bucket-shop' operations; where organisations would accept a
> customer's order and not place that order on the market. Subject
> to a number of specific exemptions, the UK regulatory regime
> requires that contracts be entered into on a regulated exchange.
> In Australia the Futures Industry Code of 1986 was largely
> designed to eliminate 'bucket shops', other fraudulent practices
> and conflicts of interest involved in transactions in futures
> contracts.

LAW REFORM ISSUES

Definitions bring a degree of certainty for market practitioners and for lawyers (who also feed well off the prevailing confusion) but an important question is what a definition provides for an investor. Adequate disclosure of what an instrument does, and its associated risks, is vital. The risk profiles of, say, a share (a security under the law) and a futures contract are different. A futures contract involves an open-ended risk and the likelihood of margining of the contract-holder. Futures trading demands constant monitoring, margining and an unknown degree of risk. That's what futures trading is all about. A sharebroker maintains a relationship with a good client but, even where that involves daily discussion, it is on a different footing to the continuous communication between futures broker and client.

There are those who argue that pigeon-holing instruments by definitions is pointless—for example, it can be argued that an ordinary share is a call option over a company's assets. But markets and their customers need some signposts.

Options muddied the water. Is an option a security or a futures contract or neither? That depends on the underlying creature over which the option is granted—and it depends where the option is traded. An option on a share issued on the ASX is a security; an option over a bank-bill futures contract on the SFE is a futures contract. An equity option granted over-the-counter, ie, between a bank and its client and not traded on an exchange, is a—what? Faced with the question, the ASC recommended that the status of options be clarified.

The Australian markets are regulated institutionally—at its simplest, what trades on ASX is a security, what trades on the SFE is a futures contract. The ASC has argued that greater attention should be paid, from the point of view of market information and risk disclosure, to the function of the instrument, ie, whether it is capital-raising (a security) and so requires a prospectus, or risk transfer/management (derivatives) which require risk disclosure. While this argument meets with considerable support, there are doubts about how it would apply in practice. Ultimately, it can be argued that almost anything can be used to manage risk.

As ever, the legislators and regulators are running to keep pace with a market whose capacity to innovate—boosted by extremely sophisticated technology—seems boundless, not least in OTC derivatives. A legislator could rule on a derivative today, only to find it had mutated into a more exotic creature next week. Given this, the ASC recommended a review of the complex regulatory and law reform issues, to ensure that products with similar functions are similarly treated, that the scope and content of the legislation properly reflects changed market circumstances and that it is sufficiently flexible to allow continuing development of new products and techniques. The ASC also recommended simplifying the regulatory regime wherever possible. The ASC identified a number of sources of concern:

- Legal uncertainty, ie, whether particular transactions are 'futures contracts' within the Corporations Law definition and, if so, whether those arranging the transactions are conducting a 'futures market'. Under the heading 'legal uncertainty' can be included issues relating to standardisation and definitions, the position of corporate treasury functions as a 'futures market', illegality under the gaming and wagering acts, retail derivative products associated with deposit or lending activities of banks and the legal enforceability of netting under the law and bankruptcy legislation.
- Different regulatory regimes applying to products with similar characteristics, eg, Chapter 8 of the Corporations Law can regulate equity swaps, commodity forwards and index options but not interest-rate swaps, commodity options or index options where a bank or merchant bank is involved on one side. The ASC has remarked on doubts about whether an OTC equity option is a futures contract, a security or neither, and whether options over interest-rate or currency forwards and swaps may be 'futures options' and therefore futures contracts. Also, eligible exchange-traded options can be traded as securities or futures, with the regulatory regime depending on the exchange on which they are traded. It has been suggested that how a product is regulated should reflect the nature of the exposures it creates rather than the particular type of instrument, an approach that challenges the existing distinction between Chapter 7 (securities) and Chapter 8 (futures).
- Protection of retail customers.
- Maintenance of orderly markets to reduce interconnecting or systemic risk. The ASC noted:

The rapid growth in the OTC derivatives market, the complexity of the risks involved and concern that both the regulatory framework and internal management controls in some institutions lagged the growth of the market, have led some overseas regulators to express concern about the potential impact of derivatives activity on interconnection or systemic risk within the financial system. There is increasing recognition that there are greater levels of interconnection between financial markets and institutions. These linkages were highlighted by the collapses of Maxwell, BCCI and Drexel Burnham & Lambert.

- Differences between the regulatory treatment of transactions on regulated exchanges and OTC markets even where these transactions involve sophisticated participants—which can disadvantage the regulated markets.
- Applying the licensing provisions of the Corporations Law to OTC activities on the grounds that licensing boosts regulatory supervision by allowing the regulatory authorities greater surveillance and monitoring of licencees' conduct.

PROPOSED REGULATORY FRAMEWORK

The ASC made eighteen recommendations for law reform, including:

- The Corporations Law should encompass all risk-management instruments, not just exchange-traded futures contracts;
- The law should distinguish between capital-raising instruments for which a prospectus is required (securities) and risk-transfer instruments for which disclosure of risk is required (regulated derivatives transactions);
- The regulatory regime should distinguish between 'securities' and 'derivatives/futures' only when there is clear reason to do so, eg, in relation to disclosure required when entering into a transaction. The ASC envisages that many of the distinctions between the regimes applying to securities and to futures, eg, those dealing with intermediaries and the regulation of markets, can be reduced or eliminated;

- Intermediaries in OTC derivatives markets should be required to be licensed, even if they are market-makers trading only as principals;
- The regime should not continue as a matter of policy to require all trading in futures contracts (derivatives) to take place on exchanges, provided that there are adequate safeguards to protect retail participants in OTC markets;
- Consideration should be given to relaxing the regulatory regime as it applies to exchange-based dealings between professional operators.

Specifically regarding OTC derivatives, the ASC proposed that an appropriate regulatory regime must take into account:

- the specific structure of derivatives markets;
- the nature of the transactions taking place in those markets;
- the risks involved in derivatives transactions; and
- the specific regulatory concerns identified in the ASC report.

Also, because domestic OTC derivatives markets are part of the large international markets, it recommended that Australia's regulatory regime be broadly consistent with that applying in major overseas jurisdictions.

Addressing a conference in July 1994, Malcolm Rodgers, ASC special policy adviser, said: 'The ASC's view is that the way the current legislation deals with futures and derivatives markets is unacceptably out-of-date. Perhaps in no other major area of the Corporations Law is there such a wide gap between what the legislative regime imagines is happening in the marketplace and what is in fact happening.' The ASC recommended a complete review of the law in this area—the task taken on by the Companies and Securities Advisory Committee (CASAC). CASAC, a committee established by statute to report to the attorney-general, is charged with guiding the reform of Australia's laws relating to derivatives. CASAC's role is to examine the recommendations proposed by the regulator, ASC. In 1994, CASAC established a special industry-based panel to assist in the daunting task of identifying and dissecting the chief issues.

NEW PRODUCTS, NEW RULES

Adding some colour to what might otherwise be a fairly arcane, although crucially influential, debate has been the push by the Australian Stock Exchange (ASX) to lift its profile in equity derivatives. Knowing only too well how long law reform can take, the ASX began snapping at the heels of the legislators in an effort to get the process moving. In January 1994 the ASX proposed amendments to the Corporations Law that would enable the listing of new equity derivatives.

The ASX had long been irritated that the primary equity derivative, a share-price index futures contract, had since 1983 been successfully traded on the Sydney Futures Exchange. It did not want to stand by and see not just the SFE but also the OTC markets capture growing business in equity derivatives. The ASX had traded call options since 1976 and more recently listed index options and warrants. But to list share futures—such as the Individual Share Futures (ISF) which began trading on the SFE in May 1994—the ASX would have to establish a futures clearing house and meet other necessary criteria relating to clearing and guaranteeing.

The proposed amendments to the Corporations Law would have broadly given the attorney-general the power to determine whether an instrument was a security or a futures contract *and* to determine which parts of either Chapter 7 or Chapter 8 applied to it. The proposal drew protest and criticism from the SFE, the Australian Financial Markets Association (AFMA) and the International Banks and Securities Association (IBSA), which cited lack of consultation and were disturbed at the implications for the OTC markets of their constituents.

The proposed amendments were withdrawn but the attorney-general, referring in parliament to the ASX's 'desire to develop a new hybrid product between a security and a future', said: 'There are real issues here about how we adequately regulate this emerging market which is neither fish nor fowl . . . maybe there needs to be some amalgam of the chapters. That will need serious debate.'

Meanwhile, ASX went ahead with plans to launch a new derivative product, a LEPO (low exercise-price option), which is a futures contract dressed as a deep in-the-money option and performing the same functions as the SFE's Individual Share Futures. Billed as a security and in the form of an option over shares, a LEPO has the risk-profile of a futures contract because the buyer is margined and, for a low entry price, gains control of a large parcel of shares.

The ASX took the view that the new product did not need specific ASC approval but the ASC wanted some assurances: was a LEPO a security or not? And, assuming it was, did existing ASX rules cope with such a product? Risk disclosure, clearing, settling, margining and the guarantee process were questions that needed clarification. The SFE watched the issue with more than passing interest, not at all happy about another organisation being allowed to offer futures without having to meet the same onerous requirements as SFE. Protracted legal challenges followed.

Exchanges locking horns is not unique to Australia. In the US, the Philadelphia Stock Exchange in 1989 listed a new product, index participations. The Chicago Mercantile Exchange put out an injunction, a federal court ruled the product a futures contract that could not be traded on a stock exchange. Index participations were withdrawn.

The US financial markets have to satisfy the Commodities and Futures Trading Commission (CFTC) and the Securities and Exchange Commission (SEC). The two often disagree. In Australia, one regulator, the ASC, enforces the Corporations Law but we have duplicated the US problem by having Chapter 7 apply to securities and Chapter 8 to futures. In the US, futures over individual shares have been banned, a move that satisfied both regulators but arguably deprived the markets of a potentially beneficial product. The objective of regulation should be efficient and well-informed markets, not just keeping regulators happy.

A revised exposure draft of amendements to the Corporations Law was issued in September 1994. The key intentions were:

- to give consideration to trading new and innovative products on Australian securities and futures exchanges on a more flexible basis than was then the case. The amendments would allow prescription by regulation of certain exchange-traded agreements under either or both of the definitions of 'securities' or 'futures contract';

- to ensure adequate regulation did not retard innovation; and
- to ensure that investors were adequately protected and that appropriate provisions applied to the trading of particular products. The agreements to be prescribed as 'securities' or 'futures contracts' would be restricted to agreements entered into on a stock exchange or a futures exchange and would not affect other markets such as over-the-counter derivatives markets.

CHAPTER 12

•••

TAX, ACCOUNTING AND DOCUMENTATION

Table 12.1 A simplified guide to the preferred tax treatment of derivatives

	ATO	Industry	Banks
Swaps			
payment in advance	due & payable	accruals	mark-to-market
payment in arrears	accruals	accruals	mark-to-market
Options (currency and interest rate)	due & payable	accruals	mark-to-market
Futures contracts	close out	accruals	mark-to-market
Swaptions	due & payable	accruals	mark-to-market

Mark-to-market is an increasingly accepted but by no means universal tax treatment of derivatives by banks around the world. The other two methods, due-and-payable and accruals, create difficulties for financial institutions. Generally, accruals has appeal for companies, while the Australian Taxation Office's insistence on due-and-payable springs from its analysis of the existing law and its wish for a simple approach.

ACCOUNTING TREATMENT OF DERIVATIVES

Accounting for financial instruments, particularly derivatives, is pioneer territory. Market practices are diverse, with some organisations choosing to leave financial instruments in the books at cost, some distinguishing between trading and hedging and some not. Also, some financial instruments are treated as off-balance-sheet and some are carried at net market value. Overall, the accounting methods used have included accrual, mark-to-market and lower of cost or market. Generally, there has been greater convergence among financial institutions than among other entities, with trading desks using mark-to-market and hedgers using the accrual method.

In 1993 came ED (exposure draft) 59. This draft standard essentially foreshadowed a shift towards market-value accounting. It requires organisations to choose either a *net market value* or *purpose-led* basis for measuring financial instruments, including derivatives. Net market value is defined for assets as the amount expected to be received from the disposal of the asset in an orderly market after deducting costs expected to be incurred in realising the proceeds of the disposal. Similarly, with liabilities, the amount expected to be paid to extinguish the liability in an orderly market, including the costs of doing so.

With the purpose-led basis, the measurement of financial assets and liabilities is based on the primary purpose for which they are intended and able to be held. Under this approach, financial instruments must be classified into three categories:

- *financing and investment financial instruments* (held to maturity or at least for the longer term) are to be reported on an accrued cost basis (except where the accrued cost is greater than net market value);
- *short-term (trading) financial instruments* are to be reported at net market value;
- *hedging financial instruments* are to be reported on the same basis as the financial and non-financial assets and liabilities being hedged.

The purpose-led basis of measurement is more subjective and leaves open the possibility of a change in intention.

ED59 addressed some long-standing accounting issues and generated vigorous debate. The bias of the draft was to record all financial instruments at market value. This would apply to financial instruments held by any entity, whether a bank or a company or other organisation. This basic thrust was in line with preferred industry practice, in that trading securities are marked to market. But the approach, the subject of heated debate worldwide, was viewed as having some pitfalls, especially for non-traded portfolios because of the difficulty of attributing a market value to something that is not traded. In the US, two recent FASB standards have suggested that a preferable alternative would be to disclose supplementary information about market value in a note to the accounts. The US requires 'available for sale' instruments, ie, those not classed as trading or financing-and-investment, to be marked to market in the balance sheet but not in the income statement—a method which shows an objectively determined measure of current value. The fluctuation is taken to a valuation reserve. This avoids unacceptable volatility in reported profits. There are those who would like to see this approach adopted in Australia on the grounds that the net-market-value approach distorts income because the reported movements are unrealised.

The concept of measuring financial instruments held for trading purposes at market value is not new, but the idea of applying market value measures to non-trading financial assets and liabilities is quite radical. This has drawn some criticism: for example, if there is no market, or if a counterparty is forced to liquidate a swap, then it cannot be assumed that an orderly market exists. Assets and liabilities are measured at each reporting date and any gain or loss arising is immediately included in the profit-and-loss account (except for hedging instruments) even though unrealised. Net market value is an objective basis of measurement. However, it has enormous implications for holders of, say, fixed-interest securities in that it could introduce a disturbing degree of volatility to reported results.

Financial assets and liabilities classed as 'financing-and-investment' can be measured on either an accrued cost or net market value basis. If accrued cost is used, ED59 requires that the financial assets must be immediately written down if net market value falls below accrued cost, even though this might be a temporary dip. The movement is unrealised and the approach conservative. If the value rises ED59 allows that to be written back up to cost through the income statement (US standards do not allow this). For example, an institution using the accrued cost method would have to provide for a fall in the market value of a bond, even if that decline in value is shortlived or the institution plans to hold the bond to maturity. Again, this introduces a worrying element of volatility into reported results.

A problem with financing-and-investment instruments is that while ED59 requires that the assets be immediately written down when net market value falls below cost, it does not allow a matching 'profit'—say, a decrease in the value of repayments to be made—on fixed-interest financing to be taken. Critics claim that this leaves the treatment one-sided. A counter-argument is to go to net market value and take the movement on both sides. But that again leads to volatility in reported income. And so the argument continues.

A financial instrument is classed as a 'hedge' when an organisation has a particular position which exposes it to risk and is holding the hedge instrument to offset that exposure. A hedge instrument is to be measured and recognised on the same basis as the position being hedged.

Under ED59, financial assets and liabilities classed as 'trading instruments' must be marked to market, which is in line with current practice.

Accounting standards for disclosure

The US, which tends to be the pacesetter in accounting standards, is emphasising a push towards greater disclosure of the details of financial instruments, including derivatives. The Australian tendency is to follow the US lead and it is likely that we will develop a standard that will be a combination of the requirements of ED59, the international exposure draft E48 and the US requirements. The US requirements include the disclosure of:

- the face, contract or notional principal amount of financial instruments with off-balance-sheet risk;
- the nature and terms of the instruments and a discussion of their credit and market risk, cash requirements, and related accounting policies;
- the accounting loss the entity would incur if any party to the financial instrument failed completely to perform according to the terms of the contract, and the collateral or other

security, if any, for the amount due proved to be of no value
to the entity; and

- the entity's policy for requiring collateral or other security
on financial instruments it accepts and a description of collateral on instruments held.

The US also requires disclosure of information about significant
concentrations of credit risk from an individual counterparty or
groups of counterparties relating to all financial instruments.
Organisations must also disclose the fair value of financial
instruments, both assets and liabilities recognised and not
recognised in the statement of financial position, where it is
practicable to estimate fair value. If not practicable, descriptive
information which would be pertinent to the value of the financial instrument should be provided.

Several major Australian banks have moved in the US direction, towards more disclosure in their annual reports, and
pressure will ensure that others, particularly if listed in the US,
follow suit. The shift reflects something of a sea-change in
attitude towards disclosure of derivatives activity, from a
drought to an abundance of information. However, to be meaningful, the details disclosed have to be understandable to the
reader and have to be comparable among the different
organisations. Also, it has been suggested that it is more explicit
to show the net risk of derivatives, ie, derivatives net of offsetting physical positions. A BIS discussion paper, *Public Disclosure
of Market and Credit Risks by Financial Intermediaries* [Fisher
report], supports the move to greater disclosure, recommending
that 'all financial intermediaries should move in the direction of
publicly disclosing periodic quantitative information which
expresses the market risks and counterparty credit risks arising
from their trading and risk-management activities, and their
performance in managing those risks'. The Fisher report pro-
poses that disclosure should:

- be meaningful, ie, express how a firm does manage risk;
- be understandable, ie, provide an adequate context for relating details to concepts;
- preserve proprietary information and not reveal specific
market opportunities and risks;

- not be burdensome—the cost of producing information should not exceed its benefit;
- be comparable;
- be verifiable, capable of being independently audited; and
- be flexible and not stifle development of risk management concepts and disclosure practices.

DOCUMENTATION

Documentation for derivatives is contained in the Aussie ISDA guide prepared by the legal firm Mallesons Stephen Jaques at the request of the Australian Financial Markets Association and in cooperation with ISDA (International Swap and Derivatives Association Inc). The guide is intended to provide uniform practices Australia-wide when dealing with a range of transactions including:

- interest-rate and currency swaps;
- interest-rate caps, collars and floors;
- forward-rate agreements;
- forward-rate bill agreements;
- swaptions;
- foreign-exchange transactions;
- currency and bond options;
- synthetic agreements for forward exchange; and
- reciprocal purchase agreements.

The introduction of the Aussie ISDA documentation brought the Australian swap market into line with international practice in documenting swaps.

Commodities

Documentation for commodities is published as a supplement (Part 19) to the 1992 Australian Guide to the AFMA/ISDA standard documentation (Australian ISDA Guide). It deals with documenting commodity transactions under the terms of the Master Agreement published by the International Swaps and Derivatives Association Inc. The supplement can be used for cash-settled or physically delivered commodity transactions including forward and spot contracts for various metals and energy commodities and options for those metals and energy contracts.

Mallesons Stephen Jaques makes the point that users of Part 19 must determine in each case whether the ISDA Master Agreement is suitable to the particular circumstances of a transaction. The firm states:

> This Part 19 is not intended to constitute a legal opinion on which users may rely in implementing actual transactions. Nor is it intended as a substitute for legal advice when documenting proposed transactions. In this regard it is strongly recommended that intending users seek prior independent professional advice in respect of the legal, taxation, stamp duty and financial institutions duty implications arising from the use of the ISDA Master Agreement. This Part 19 is intended as an aid in understanding issues which arise under Australian laws when the ISDA Master Agreement is used.

Australian Addendum Number 11—Commodity Transactions

Parties to commodity transactions who incorporate Australian Addendum Number 11—Commodity Transactions (an addendum to the ISDA Master Agreement) agree that every commodity transaction between them subsequently entered into is a transaction governed by the terms of the addendum and the ISDA Master Agreement. Such commodity transactions can be confirmed in various ways including by telex, letter, Reuters direct dealing system, Telerate trading service or facsimile.

The 1994 International Bullion Master Agreement

Compiled by the London Bullion Market, the British Bankers' Association and representatives of the US's Financial Markets Lawyers Group, the International Bullion Master Agreement (IBMA) builds on the experience gained in drafting earlier foreign-exchange master agreements such as the International Currency Options Market Master Agreement (ICOM) and the International Foreign Exchange Master Agreement (IFEMA). IBMA aims to provide a common set of terms for spot and forward bullion trades and bullion options in the international bullion market. As with all master agreements, the objective is to reduce trading risks and the costs to market participants of negotiating bilateral agreements.

IBMA is published in two versions, one governed by English law and one by New York law.

Repos

Each repo transaction is agreed individually. The repo interest rate is determined when the repo is initiated, as is the agreed repurchase price. Where a repo is not 'open-ended', ie, on demand, the sellback/buyback date is agreed at the outset of the transaction. When this date arrives the counterparties decide whether the transactions are to be rolled over or terminated.

There are two documents endorsed by AFMA:

- *Memorandum of Agreed Terms and Conditions*, prepared for AFMA by the legal firm Corrs Chambers Westgarth, deals exclusively with reciprocal purchase agreements and is recommended for use with clients whose only trading relationship is through the repo market.
- *ISDA Master Agreement*, prepared by the legal firm Mallesons Stephen Jaques for AFMA and ISDA (International Swaps and Derivatives Association), which can also be used for repos if Addendum Number 9—Reciprocal Purchase Agreement—is included.

Advantages in using the ISDA Master Agreement include providing participants with the choice of using one master agreement for all transactions, including swaps, options, FRAs and repos; using one master agreement simplifies documentation; and it gives the option of specifying net payments for corresponding payment dates for all transactions, reducing settlement costs and risks. With all transactions regulated by the same agreement, the amount payable on early termination will be payable by reference to aggregate net exposures under all transactions and therefore would not exclude amounts payable in connection with repos. By incorporating Addendum Number 9 in the ISDA Master Agreement, the parties agree that every repo between them is governed by the agreement, whether or not its confirmation refers to the Master Agreement or Addendum Number 9 and whether or not the parties state in their confirmation that the repo is governed by the terms of any other master agreement.

There is no standard documentation for securities lending; agreements are arranged between individual parties.

INDEX
· · · · · · · ·